Far...Beyond the Starry Sky

Second Edition

Vernal E. Richardson

ISBN 978-1-68570-664-7 (paperback)
ISBN 978-1-68570-665-4 (digital)

Christian Faith Publishing
832 Park Avenue
Meadville, PA 16335
www.christianfaithpublishing.com

Printed in the United States of America

In memory of Teena (Elpha Ernestine Patton) Richardson.

Contents

A charming memoir that reflects on the author's life as a musician, teacher, pilot, and family man.

Richardson's debut effort was inspired by friends who told him to document his long, fascinating life. Now retried in the North Georgia mountains, he grew up as the son of farmers during a time when the country was strangled by the Depression. Richardson began teaching himself the violin at an early age. After his father noticed his precocious talent, he insisted his son take private lessons. That marked the beginning of a successful career both as a musician and as an academic. Richardson eventually earned his doctorate in violin from Catholic University and taught in serval well-regarded music departments across the US. He also played on an impressive number of famous recordings, solidifying a legacy as a virtuosic performer. The narrative, however, follows much more than Richardson's professional life; a professed patriot, he was also a military pilot. Adding some drama to his reflections, he recounts a harrowing experience flying a B-47 during a training exercise gone frighteningly wrong. The recollection includes ruminations on a tumultuous period in American history: Richardson share is encounter with racism in New Orleans in 1963 and then at a predominantly black high school in Atlanta where he taught. Sometimes he digresses too far from the main narrative, as when he broaches the topic of sex education in the US. But his original ideas redeem the lengthy asides: "For further consideration of sexual and musical symbolism we could study the famous Rite of Spring by Igor Stravinsky. Study the shapes mentioned, the sounds, the rhythms, the melodies, the dance movements, and the story." His candor is notable too; he confesses to being tempted by a fourteen-year-old girl while a full-grown man. The reader is left wishing for more about his family life, which is somewhat neglected. But the remembrances remain sweet, forthcoming, and sometimes poignant.

A cheerful depiction of a life well-lived and gratefully recounted.

Kirkus Reviews

Foreword

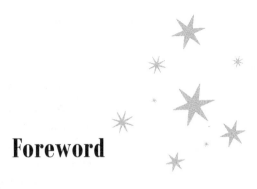

I was fortunate to be able to attend the Herbert Blomstedt Conducting Institute at Loma Linda University, Riverside, California, during the summer of 1982. (Maestro Blomstedt was the conductor of the San Francisco Symphony. One of his first sentences to workshop participants was "I am a Christian." I knew that Loma Linda is sponsored by the Seventh-Day Adventists, but I had never before known a professional symphony conductor whose life and work were dedicated to Jesus Christ.)

In a subsequent lecture Mr. Blomstedt made another statement that affected me greatly: "You cannot *make* a career in music. If you *have* a career, it is because someone *gave* it to you." I realized that a multitude of people have contributed to my career. How could I thank them?

I have been teaching for more than half a century, during which time I have amassed a collection of personal experiences that I use as stories to illustrate material I am teaching. It would be convenient if these stories were collected in a publication. Perhaps I could simply refer to a chapter rather than telling time-consuming stories during lessons.

Many of my friends are amazed when I tell them that I played violin on sessions when some of their favorite music was recorded. (These were recorded on LPs more than fifty years ago: they were recently re-released in the form of CDs. Almost every year, several movies include extracts from "our" tapes in their soundtracks. I no longer am surprised when I hear our recordings during television programs.) When I describe the conditions under which we made recordings in those days my friends say, "You must write a book about this!" So I decided to write this book.

I have often said that retirement is a time to reflect upon life and to try to make sense of it. In the rush of daily existence during a working career, it is often difficult to make sense of seemingly random events. When I began writing, I soon recognized that this book threatened to become a library! I decided to include only material that contributed positively to my development as a musician. Other materials might become future books. I also tried to describe disparate events in the order of their *occurrence*. Even with the risk of confusion, I feel that this helps the reader to empathize with the emotions I experienced at the time.

Thanks to my good friend Louise Sherman for proofreading and making suggestions about this book. If any faults are found(!), *please blame her.*

Vernal E. Richardson

1

The first event I can remember happened when I was two years old. I can reconstruct this because during the event, I heard one of my sisters cry. She was one of a set of twins (Wilma Sue and Wanda Lou) born when I was age two.

We were living in the Brock House, named after the family who had owned it for generations. It was a combination of Cape Cod and Center-Hall Colonial, said to be at least one hundred years old. If this is true, the house was probably built about 1830, well before the Civil War. It was well-built mostly of yellow poplar, but it was in terrible condition. It had no foundation as such, being built upon large corner-stones. It had been painted at some time, but the paint was peeling in intricate, somehow decorative, patterns of white against the fibrous gray of weathered wood. There was no electricity and no indoor plumbing. Our drinking water came from a very old white-washed stone springhouse about fifty yards from the kitchen door. The water was icy even in summer, and there was an arrangement of stones to support containers of butter, milk, and other foods that needed refrigeration. Our bathwater came from Shuffle Creek, so named because of the sound it made rushing over its bed of stones. We carried all our water in buckets.

The spring-house was built into a hill so that we could climb onto its roof simply by walking around the building. In late summers, Bea and Mary Jean, my two older sisters, often would climb with me to the roof and lie on it under the shade of enormous beech trees. We would take bottles of spring water and twigs of beech limbs with nuts on them ready to eat. As we enjoyed the delicious (but labor-intensive) snack we would pretend we were at an exclusive restaurant with famous people, drinking wine and eating exotic delicacies.

The house was quite picturesque, situated beside a heavily-timbered hill. Some of the trees (elms, butternuts, yellow poplar) later succumbed to various diseases and disappeared. Meadow flowers, flowering shrubs, blackberries, raspberries, and rambling roses grew profusely wherever there was room. A curved limestone road ran in front of the house. The road had rather recently replaced the nearby Shuffle Creek, which had served as a makeshift highway for horses, buggies, and wagons. When cars became popular it was necessary to build a road.

There was little traffic past our house at that time. We were in the middle of the Great Depression, and people could hardly afford to joyride. (We purchased gasoline at the local grocery store, where we would pump the fuel into a glass tank with moveable markers to show how much fuel was there. I have often seen people buy one gallon of gasoline for about fifteen cents.) In fact, people could hardly afford to live. Money was very scarce, and the economy was largely based upon barter, credit, and charity. The word *charity* was not used: we were just being "neighborly."

Doctors made house-calls routinely. Dr. Batman was expected to provide our medical care when needed, and he made the six-mile trip from Bloomington (Indiana) to Unionville as necessary for many years. (Children were born at home. I never heard of a hospital birth in those days. In fact, most old folks were very much afraid of hospitals. They thought of them as places to go and die.)

Of course, I was not aware of any of this at age two. My memory recorded a night when the house was dark with an inky blue darkness punctuated randomly by globes of bright gold light from kerosene lamps. Years later, I saw a painting by Van Gogh *(The Starry Night)* that recalled this memory vividly.

I saw a hairy hand pushing my shirt sleeve up while another matching hairy hand rubbed something cold and wet on my arm. In the distance, I heard one of the twins cry. The second hairy hand came into view again, this time holding a syringe, which looked almost as large as my arm. Then I felt the sting of the needle as it punctured my arm. I heard the voice, which I would come to identify as that of Dr. Batman, "Just a touch of pneumonia."

As I recall the pneumonia experience and its later association with the Van Gogh painting, I remember other experiences that seem to suggest that humans (and perhaps some animals) have universal consciousness. We seem to have an inherited awareness of common human experience sometimes hundreds, perhaps thousands of years old. Richard Wagner was perhaps thinking of this phenomenon when he composed the famous opera *The Flying Dutchman*. Near the beginning of the opera when the Dutchman sees Senta for the first time he meditates "as from the mists of times' forgotten ages this blessed vision speaks to me." Senta has similar experiences as she sees an ancient portrait of the Dutchman, who apparently has visited the same home earlier, searching for the woman who would be faithful to him and release him from his curse.

Perhaps universal consciousness explains the mysterious child prodigy, who, at the age of two, seems to already know how to play the violin and is able to "learn" how to play complex compositions just by being "reminded" by his/her teacher. Such children sometimes can perform at the age of five or six years complete violin concertos with excellent memory, intonation, technique, and style (not to mention complete confidence and security). At rehearsals, they often require babysitters to care for their ordinary childish needs. Mrs. Rudolph Kratina, my landlady when I was in the Atlanta Symphony (1955), served in that capacity when Yehudi Menuhin performed a Mozart Concerto with the Dresden Philharmonic at age seven. (Mr. Kratina was the principal cellist at Dresden with conductor-composer Richard Strauss at the time.)

Could universal consciousness also explain such mysteries as the swallows' "return to Capistrano"? How can gnats and other small flying insects whose life span is measured in hours or days learn to see and avoid being swatted by humans? How do homing pigeons find their way from military trenches in France across the English Channel to London? Why has the human race singled out as a masterpiece Edvard Munch's painting *The Primal Scream* from among thousands of superficially similar paintings of the same era? What do we mean by the words *Zeitgeist? Déjà vu? (Irish) second sight? Extra-sensory perception?* Why do similar inventions and scientific discoveries occur at the same time in widely separated locations whose populations have little ability to communicate? How does universal consciousness relate to intimations of eternity? I don't know the answers to these questions, but I have had many experiences that I cannot explain without reference to universal consciousness.

In my community, Gypsies, would often park their horse-drawn, brightly decorated covered wagons in empty fields or lots, remaining there for a period of time before moving to a new location. Gypsies had a rather unsavory reputation for petty thievery and annoying behavior. They were neither enthusiastically welcomed nor sadly missed in their comings and goings.

Parents sometimes threatened their children when they behaved badly. "I'll give (or sell) you to the Gypsies if you don't behave yourself!" Children seemed not to realize that the Gypsies might not want them: they had an overabundance of children already.

A story circulated generally in our community: several members of the community were walking along a country lane when they were approached by a Gypsy caravan travelling at high speed with horses galloping. It stopped and allowed a young child from the walking group to get aboard the wagon (members of our community thought this was prophetic). Then it galloped away amid blowing dust, which seemed to have the appearance of flames, perhaps due to the angle of the sun at that time of day. After traveling a short distance it seemed to lift into the air, evaporate, and disappear. One of the children in the community died a few days later. The image of the flying horse must have remained in my subconscious, waiting to be recalled years later when I was in college.

2

For some reason, probably related to the Great Depression, in 1935 we moved from the Brock House north of Unionville to a two-room tar-paper house owned by my mother's half-brother Virgil. I was three years old, and I can remember some details vividly.

The floor was partially covered by linoleum so badly worn that there was little of the original design left. Cracks in the floor allowed cold air to enter, and there was no foundation to help block it. There was a combination living/bedroom and a combination kitchen/dining area. A wood-burning heater was in the living/bedroom and a wood-burning cooking range was in the kitchen. There was no electricity, no plumbing, and no water inside the house. All our water had to be carried from Uncle Virgil's well several hundred feet away from our house. This primitive style of living was not unusual in our neighborhood at that time. We were trying to live through the Depression, which came upon the heels of our version of the Industrial Revolution. President Franklin Delano Roosevelt had been in office about three years, and our country was in economic recovery, but progress was slow in the Unionville community.

Apparently, the tenants who lived in Uncle Virgil's house before we moved in had developed a rather prosperous enterprise. We had been living in the house for only a short time when one night, after dark, we heard a knock on the front door. My father took his flashlight and looked out to see a man standing on the porch with a glass jug in his hand. As soon as the man saw my father, he left without a word. This happened several times. We assumed that some people were accustomed to buying "moonshine" from the previous tenants and didn't know they had left. The going price for "moonshine," also known as "white lightening," was $1.25 per gallon.

My father, Edgar, was the son of Howard and Nancy Richardson, rather prosperous farmers who lived on Getty's Creek, a few miles south of Unionville. They were well adjusted to life as farmers, and their economy involved very little cash. They grew most of their food on their rich little farm, including vegetables, fruit, and meat. Their cellar was filled with canned fruit and vegetables, pickles, jellies, preserves, and relishes. They slaughtered their own pork and beef and preserved the meat in time-honored ways. They kept a few milk cows, which supplied them with dairy products. They grew their own grain, made flour or meal, and baked their own bread. They attended church services every Sunday morning, driving their horse and buggy. After services, they would eat the lunch they had brought and drive back home in time to milk their cows. They were quite surprised when a few factories were built in nearby Bloomington, and they were even more surprised when the factory owners began to hire young men to work on the production lines. My father was one of those who were hired.

Showers Furniture Factory, where my father worked, hired young men for the production line and paid them on the basis of "piece-work," meaning that pay was based upon the amount of work done. The workers were motivated to do as much work as possible, often without considering the quality of their work.

Since they repeated the same operations day after day for eight or more hours, they learned to work astonishingly fast. Soon, my father was bringing home more money than his parents had ever seen. The family quickly developed the attitude that prosperity would grow at an increasing rate for the indefinite future. They had no idea that the market for Showers Furniture could ever become saturated. Also, some of the farmwork was neglected because of the new priority of factory work.

Soon after as my parents were married and beginning to have children, the Great Depression arrived. (My sister "Bea" was born on May 20, 1927, the day Charles Lindberg made his famous flight to Paris, France.) There was little or no work available, and pay was very low. Men stood in line each morning at the stone quarry, hoping to pound stone with a sledgehammer for seventy-five cents per day. Experienced farm workers would plow all day with a team of horses for one dollar plus the noon meal. Factory work, which had shown much promise, disappeared because most people could not afford to buy factory-made products.

My father tried to grow a garden near our house. There was a good-sized plot, but it was clay. Dad broke the soil with a push-plow (often called a "hunch-plow"), and I carried water in a gallon bucket to water plants as he set them out. There was little organic material in the soil, so the predictable happened: the plants withered and died under the withering sun. This was only one of many defeats that my parents suffered, but I never heard them complain. With great courage and energy, they simply tried every kind of work imaginable to survive and provide for their family of (eventually) six children. They dug, dried, and sold ginseng and May-apple roots to companies, which made them into medicine (ironically meant to serve as aphrodisiacs). During the winter, my dad hunted for possums, coons, foxes, mink, and muskrat to cure their pelts and sell them as fur. Our diet included fish, squirrel, rabbit, pheasant, quail, and sometimes raccoon. We ate few chickens since we needed eggs.

My parents would not be considered educated in the present era. My mother graduated high school, and my father completed "common school" (eighth grade) plus two years of high school. Along with this small amount of formal education, they learned an informal code of behavior from their parents and the community:

1. Be clean. No matter what else was happening, my mother did her laundry on Monday each week. The next day, she did the ironing, and the following day, she was usually sick from overwork. I still have one of her "hand-irons," heavy metal boat-shaped implements that she heated on the stove summer and winter. The wood handle is removable so that she could have could have several irons heating while the one in use was cooling. I watched her many times as she worked to keep her family clean and presentable. I

wondered why her hands felt rough as she rubbed Vicks VapoRub on my chest and back when I had a cold. Her hands were rough, but her iron-handle is smooth. I remember when it was newly purchased from Thrasher Hardware in Bloomington. The edges were sharp and splintery. It was finished in a clear lacquer. Printed in ink is "30 C," probably its price. The wood is now a red-brown color, the result of many years of heating and soaking with perspiration. It is worth more than thirty cents now!

2. Also, be clean. Our code included bathing, perhaps not every day, but often enough and thoroughly, enough to fill the requirement. Our soap was strong enough to remove a layer of skin along with the dirt. *Perhaps we were doing preventive bathing?* During winter months, we carried bathwater, heated it, bathed in the tin laundry tub, and emptied it for the next person. I have to admit that when we were younger, we often shared the same water.

3. Be honest. Our word was our bond. We didn't know about written contracts and lawsuits. In fact, we knew Bible verses, which seemed to advise against any kind of action at law. We were careful not to lie, and anyone who had the reputation of dishonesty was shunned by the community.

4. Be generous. We gave to those who asked. During the Depression, many people would come to our door day or night to ask for food. They were never turned away empty-handed, even though this might create a hardship for our family.

5. Go to church whenever the doors are open unless "providentially hindered." Several times each year, we would have "all-day meetin' with dinner on the ground." This meant morning worship, picnic lunch, afternoon "singin'" and evening worship. I have known people who would cross Bean Blossom Creek when it was flooded and dangerous in order to get to prayer meeting. The method was practical and rather ingenious: dismount from the horse, remove all clothing and put it in a protective bag, put the horse in the

water and hold onto its tail to cross the creek, dress again, mount the horse, and ride on to church.

6. Be independent. "Owe no man anything." We would often refuse offered help because we didn't want to feel obliged to repay. When we did accept help, our way of saying "thank-you" was "much obliged," pronounced "much *obleeged.*" We were not comfortable until we had found a way to repay the kindness. This attitude made acceptance of new government programs slow and difficult. The programs included Social Security, distribution of free food "com-modities," CCC camp, and WPA.

CCC camp was meant to provide employment and simple living for men who couldn't find work. The employment consisted of construction projects such as dams and roads, cutting timber, and other labor-intensive activities. The living conditions were rather like those found in army camps. WPA was a system of employment for men who remained at home but worked on local projects such as building roads. Often, the men seemed to be doing little, which led to disparaging remarks about "leaning on their shovels and collecting money from the taxpayers." When I heard these remarks, they were usually made by men who had no shovels to lean upon and who didn't pay income taxes.

3

Our community began to recover from the Depression in 1936. Showers Furniture Factory began operating again, and my father was recalled to work. He was able to buy a 1929 Model "A" Ford two-door sedan, still in rather good condition, although considered worn-out according to the standards of the time. We moved back to the Brock house, which we liked very much, especially in comparison to Uncle Virgil's little tar-papered house.

The workers at Showers, probably in an effort to avoid recurrent unemployment, decided to join the CIO (Congress of Industrial Organizations), one of the most popular unions at that time. This led to a "strike," something none of us had known before. The strike involved many hours of standing in a "picket line" to prevent non-union workers ("scabs") from operating the factory. There was danger involved, with some scuffling and outright fighting. There were rumors that the CIO was a communistic organization and a threat to the freedom of the community. We also heard vague references to the Nazis in Germany and Italy and the speculation that there could be another world war soon. Our family was alone many nights while Dad was in the picket line, and we were afraid that someone would attack us in our home. It was winter, and often, a cold rain was falling. Trying to stay warm, the strikers burned wood and trash in a barrel. I would lie awake at home worrying about Dad. Our coonhound, living under the house, would bark and howl mournfully for hours every night. Eventually the strike was settled, and our family enjoyed the first relatively peaceful and prosperous period of our existence.

Professor Knecht of Indiana University began a new enterprise that our community had never known before. He built modest but attractive homes and sold them with no down payment. A purchaser could live with his family in the home and pay for it like rent, eventually owning it. To us, this was the realization of a dream! My parents bought one of the homes, a Cape Cod frame house, only three years old. As I recall, it cost fifteen hundred dollars with about four acres of land. Typically for that time, there was no electricity, no telephone, no plumbing, and no water available on the premises. We moved in immediately with great enthusiasm.

Getty's Creek ran through our property. It was rather wide with a sandstone bottom and grassy banks about four feet high. The creek came out of the surrounding hills, so there was a lot of "fall." (When we had heavy rainfall, the creek filled quickly to flood stage, and the water ran rapidly and deep, a flash flood.) Usually, the creek ran in the middle between the banks and was about one foot deep. It was an attractive place for playing or swimming, and Mom found it useful as a place to do laundry.

My sisters and I carried water from the creek to an improvised fireplace on the bank. We filled a large kettle with water and burned wood for heat. Then we filled a hand-operated washing machine (from Sears & Roebuck) with boiling water, added soap and laundry, and washed by operating a dasher with the long handle that protruded from the end of the machine. It was labor-intensive but effective. Being about ten years old, I was ideal to provide power to operate the machine.

One hot summer day, we prepared the laundry as usual. My sister Mary Jean and I were sharing the work of operating the washing machine when one of its legs sank into the soft dirt. Immediately, the top-heavy machine tipped over, catching me just below the waist and knocking me down. The boiling water poured over my back from the knees up, filling the pockets of my jeans. I was face-down in the dirt and couldn't move until the machine became lighter as the water emptied. The pain was unimaginable! I saw Mom as she ran over to me, lifted the machine, and stood me up. She quickly removed my jeans, and I saw huge blisters forming on my legs and stomach. Mom told my sisters to run over to Theodore Kerr's house next door and ask him to drive us to Dr. Batman's office in Bloomington. (Theodore owned and operated our school bus.) He arrived after a few minutes and placed me on my hands and knees in the front seat of the bus where the windshield defroster fan could cool my back and hips. I remember being embarrassed because I was naked! We probably broke a few speeding laws on our trip to Bloomington.

When we arrived at Dr. Batman's office, I ran to the door and was met by one of the nurses. She immediately escorted me to the treatment room where Dr. Batman and his assistants treated my burns and wrapped me in bandages from my knees to my chin. The pain had abated somewhat, and suddenly, I was very sleepy. I learned later that I was probably in shock and near death.

Somehow, it was decided that I must go to Bloomington Hospital for further treatment, and I went by ambulance. I don't remember much about the trip except the sound of the siren. When we arrived, I could hardly believe how good it felt to lie down on the hospital bed. I am sure that I must have been under sedation by that time.

My principal nurse was Ms. Reistika (spelling doubtful). I remember it partly because my sisters and I promptly dubbed her Ms. Rice Sticker, but also because she was a very kind, understanding, sympathetic, helpful nurse. I needed those qualities badly.

I spent the next week unconscious, probably in induced coma. My parents told me later that Dr. Batman informed them that he had done all he could for me and that I was likely to die. My dad told Dr. Batman that he should try anything that showed any likelihood of helping me, regardless of cost or inconvenience. My mom was told that if I lived, I certainly would never walk again, but she could try exercising my legs to keep the tendons from becoming attached. My mom was instructed how to move my legs, and she did a routine of exercise several times each day. It is almost certain that the combined extra treatment and exercises tipped the scales in the direction of my survival and ability to perform normal activities later.

Dr. Batman believed that for my burns to heal properly, he would need to remove my bandages each morning, pulling the necrotic tissue off in the process. This was done at 10:00 a.m. daily, a short time after breakfast. The pain of removal approached that of the original accident, and I remember dreading to see the door open at that time. I don't believe they gave me any type of pain medication, and I can recall beginning to cry before they started working and screaming uncontrollably during the process. I also remember the doctor applying various types and colors of ointments to different areas of burns, perhaps related to the degree of the burn in each area. A small wooden paddle was used to apply the ointments, and I remember the pain as the paddles were scraped on my flesh during the application. The medication used most was called "gentian violet."

Dr. Batman discussed the possibility that skin grafts might be necessary. Skin grafting was described to me, and I was understandably relieved when it was decided that this would not be done.

Our community was praying for me and my family, especially during the time when I was unconscious. I was told later that I said some very prophetic things while unconscious, sounding as though speaking from heaven. Many of my friends believed that I was sharing divine revelations with them and that my life would be spared because I had much left to do on earth.

After three weeks in the hospital, I was released to go home. I was not allowed out of bed for another week. I assumed that I could walk easily, so when the time came, I simply stepped out of bed and fell on the floor! I had forgotten how to walk, and I had to learn all over again. This was quite a shock, but I learned quickly. Somehow, I managed to start school and resume all the activities that had been suspended during the four or five weeks since my accident. My family gave me a wind-up toy boat (yellow enameled metal), and my aunt Ethel (Dad's sister) gave me my first pocket knife, a very small yellow-handled Camillus brand. (It has no *spade* blade. That would come when I was older.) I often played with the boat in the creek near the site where I was burned. I still have these gifts packed away in a box of mementos from childhood years.

My parents had to assume a debt of approximately three hundred dollars for my treatment and hospital stay. This amounted to about ten weeks wages for Dad, whose pay was approximately thirty dollars per week. We had not heard of health insurance at that time.

4

According to the sign over the front door, the Unionville Church of Christ was founded in 1820, four years after Indiana became a state. My family worshipped there "every time the door was open, unless providentially hindered." This was the attitude and practice of our community, and it involved quite a lot of effort and determination.

In much of our community, there were no real roads, only paths that had been followed by pedestrians, horses, and buggies before cars were available. Many members of the community owned cars by the time I was born: Model A Fords, 1928 or 1929 Chevrolets, an occasional Dodge, Pontiac, or Buick. I remember a Lincoln that a neighbor bought for fifty dollars to make the engine and chassis into a sawmill. It was like new when he bought it, but its owner couldn't afford to drive it because of excess gasoline consumption. These cars would mire down into the mud when the road wasn't frozen in winter, sometimes dragging the frame or losing traction completely. I don't believe I saw a new car until about 1936, and they were rare then.

Our church was organized in the pattern of the New Testament, with elders and deacons as leaders. Women were not allowed as leaders, following the biblical injunction that said, "Let your women keep silence in the churches." There were no pastors, but we had travelling evangelists who visited on schedule, usually once per month. Sometimes we would have several evangelists on schedules that allowed us to have preachers every week. When no preacher was present, the men of the congregation would read and comment upon the scripture of the week. We studied the Holy Bible rather systematically, one chapter each week when there was no preacher. During my childhood, we studied the entire Bible several times. Some chapters were not very meaningful to us ("Abraham begat Isaac and Isaac begat Jacob"), but we studied them dutifully just the same, the reader often interjecting comments ("How true that is!") between phrases.

Visiting evangelists were almost always uneducated. Our community distrusted education along with most intellectual activity, perhaps because Indiana University was just a few miles away in Bloomington. They had seen or heard rumors of the behavior of IU students and faculty, and they wanted no part of it (even though a number of them worked at the University in a variety of jobs).

When an evangelist was present, we had services on Saturday night, Sunday morning, and Sunday evening. Some Sundays we had all-day meeting with dinner on the ground.

Sermons usually included some variation of the "Gospel Plan of Salvation," with touches of originality provided by the evangelists. Often charts and drawings accompanied the sermons, drawn or painted in the style of medieval art. (I would love to have some of these now. They might be interesting examples of primitive painting.) The subject was familiar to the congregation: Humanity is lost in sin and can be redeemed only by following a pattern derived from the New Testament. The pattern is: hearing (the Gospel), belief, repentance, confession, and baptism. There were ample scriptures illustrating the acceptable manner of accomplishing these works. After baptism, converts were to go into the world and convert more sinners.

Sermons were usually presented in a fiery, almost hysterical manner. I remember Preacher Timmons from Illinois. As I recall, he drove a 1936 Chevrolet, the newest car I had seen at that time. He was a farmer in Illinois, but he travelled as an evangelist at times. He usually wore bib overalls with a dress coat and tie. This was a rather common manner of dressing for the relatively prosperous man in our community.

Preacher Timmons preached long sermons with much angry shouting and fist-pounding on the lectern. Young children like me were expected to sit and listen without going to sleep, although some *did* sleep (I don't know how). At the end of his sermons, Preacher Timmons always called for repentant sinners to come forward during the song of invitation.

The singing! We had only unaccompanied vocal music, but the congregation took seriously the responsibility to "sing and make melody in your heart to God." The Brock family was known for good singing. Martin Brock was our leader. He had a very high tenor voice, which I would call a counter-tenor today. He could easily sing into the soprano range with beautiful tone and excellent intonation. Other members of his family sang soprano, alto, and bass, providing leadership for the rest of the congregation. In addition, Craig (Mrs. Leslie) Peters, a fine soprano who had studied voice at Indiana University School of Music, was often present. At times, the entire congregation sounded like a trained chorus. I have often wondered if the tradition of excellent singing came to us somehow from the Welsh, immortalized in the great movie *How Green Was My Valley*.

We sang hymns from the hymnal *Great Songs of the Church*, a collection of fine hymns with solid theological foundation (and *shaped notes*). I memorized many of the hymns, and I carried a verse of "Thou, My Everlasting Portion" in my wallet for years, until it wore out: "*Not for ease or worldly pleasure, Nor for fame my prayer shall be. Gladly will I toil and suffer, Only let me walk with Thee.*" These sentiments guided me through high school, college, professional violin playing, and Air Force service.

Walking with Jesus! The idea was born mostly in response to the singing in church when I was a small boy. One of the hymns we frequently sang ("Sweetly, Lord, Have We Heard Thee Calling") had as its refrain "*Footprints of Jesus that make the pathway glow. We will follow the steps of Jesus where'er they go.*" Many of our hymns echoed this idea, and I meditated upon this theme sometimes during the sermons. I remember that I once saw a vision while meditating.(At the front of our building was a sort of carved wooden arch with brackets for hanging the kerosene lamps that lighted the pulpit. The arch had ornamental symbols carved into it, and it was stained dark brown and varnished attractively.)

As Preacher Timmons ranted on and on, I saw what seemed to be a pathway ascending from the arch toward heaven. The pathway was made of gold filigree, similar to the designs of Moorish art (which I had not seen at that time), and between the abstract figures of gold was something like pearls or mother-of-pearl. The pathway curved upward in an artistic design representing the steps of Jesus. At that moment, I knew that I wanted to be baptized and to follow Jesus.

(This was not encouraged by our congregation for theological reasons, which I accepted at the time, but later, I wondered how they originated.)

The doctrine: When a person is baptized, all sin is forgiven and washed away. At that moment, the person is perfect, saved, and ready to enter heaven. If the person willfully sins afterward, there is no forgiveness since baptism can be done only once.

Our community had a serious problem. The people loved basketball. They also loved Jesus, perhaps more than they loved basketball. Playing basketball was (in their judgement) "riotous living," condemned in the Bible and therefore sinful. It was unreasonable to expect a high school student *not* to play basketball; therefore, it was wise to postpone baptism until after graduation from high school (going to college was not considered a possibility). Adults could attend basketball games, but if they were baptized, they were not encouraged to sit in the section of the audience where cheering for the team was done.

Our congregation had many more theological difficulties but perhaps one is enough to illustrate the confusion and conflict I experienced while growing up.

Our church was equipped to give guidance to children. We were taught by example a code of human behavior that served the community fairly well. We lived in a closed circle socially, and outside influence was not welcome. Our functions were clearly defined in terms of masculine and feminine roles. We had a very rigid "pecking order." We had enough education to survive and to function in a small agrarian community. We didn't have adequate preparation to deal with the new world, which was coming to us within a few years.

Our building was very old, a small wooden structure with cornerstones (no solid foundation). We were told that the original building was a log cabin, and that two of the walls were kept and extended with wood framing to make the building about four times as large as the original. Later, when the building was torn down to build a new one, the log walls were rediscovered. A small entry area led to the larger room where the congregation worshipped. There was only one entry door, but the inside room had two aisles (three rows of benches).

We had no water supply. Two privies stood at the back of the building, and the congregation tried to avoid using them.

There was no electricity. Lighting was basically a kerosene system that supported several ceiling fixtures through pipes. Pressure was provided by pumping an air tank with a tire pump. When the deacon (Joe Chitwood) lighted the lights, he would use corncobs soaked in kerosene to heat the wicks to incandescence. He would climb up on the pews and place the lighted cobs under the wicks to heat them.

Heat was provided by a very large potbellied stove, which our song-leader kept filled with wood during services. A long stovepipe hanging from bailing-wire brackets extended from the stove to the chimney at the back of the room. The fact that the building never caught on fire could have been sufficient proof of miracles.

The pews were made of yellow poplar, a light, strong wood that was plentiful at the time the building was constructed. The boards were wide and long enough to construct each pew of basically two pieces with bracing, supports, and trim on the edges. Poplar had also the advantage that it was easy to carve, and the men fell into the habit of carving the pews.

In our community, practically all men carried pocket knives. Most of the men were farmers, and pocket knives filled many sorts of utilitarian needs. In addition, men were likely to pull out their knives at odd moments when they were not working. They would either sharpen the knives or whittle with them. The knife blades were usually razor-sharp, particularly the spade blade.

The spade blade was a rather short blade with a triangular-shaped tip. All edges of this blade were sharp. The blades were used primarily for castrating baby pigs, a chore that all farmers had to do. (After castrating the pigs, their teeth were cut out using wire-cutter pliers. This was done so that the mother sow would allow them to suckle.) Spade blades were also good for carving the backs of church pews. The back two rows of pews in our church were practically destroyed with carvings, some of which were rather ingenious. (When ancient paintings were discovered in caves, they reminded me of the bench carvings in my church.)

Even though our church believed in spontaneity in prayers and sermons, we developed our own rituals. Our prayers were almost identical week after week, and most prayer leaders carefully avoided changing them. If a new phrase was included in a prayer, it would be noticed and discussed privately. If word got around that it was acceptable, it would be adopted by other prayer leaders, and eventually, it would become a part of the permanent ritual.

One of our rituals has always interested me: our young men would gather in front of the church before services, talking and often smoking cigarettes. They would wait until the first hymn had begun, and then they would form two lines and march in, stubbing their cigarettes on the door-frame as they entered the building. They strutted as though attempting to impress someone, perhaps the young ladies. They would march to the back seats (always kept empty for them), where they would be seated, ready to begin the morning carving.

5

Peters and Wampler Barber Shop was located on the square in Bloomington, in the basement below Kahn's Shoe Store. It was the favorite barber shop in Bloomington, and everyone I knew went there for haircuts. Both barbers gave careful attention to the needs and desires of their customers.

The shop had four chairs, each with its sink and a counter filled with bottles of shampoo and hair tonic. In addition, there was a shower in the bathroom and a shoe-shine stand near the front of the shop. For fifty cents, a man could have a shower before he had a haircut and/or shave. There were no women customers, only men and boys. Occasionally, women would bring their young boys for haircuts, often first haircuts. These were emotional occasions for the women as well as the boys. There was no air-conditioning, but several ceiling fans helped to keep the temperature endurable during summer months. Haircuts cost $1.25, shaves approximately the same, and shoe-shines were fifteen cents. Tipping was allowed, but it was rather infrequent.

One Saturday, when I was about ten years old, I went for a haircut. The shoe-shine boy, the eleven-year-old son of one of the owners of Carter and O'Haver Drug Store, was not there. Mr. Peters (known as "Pete" to us) told me that the boy had to be circumcised (I knew about circumcision from the many references to it in the Bible), and that he didn't plan to return to his job. Immediately, I thought that could be an opportunity for me! I asked about it and was told that the responsibilities included sweeping hair-clippings off the floor, preparing and cleaning the shower, and shining shoes. I would be paid for shining shoes, and I would be given any tips from the shower duties. I thought the job sounded attractive, even though I had never shined a shoe before that time.

I began work on Monday, after buying shoe-shining supplies from City Hat and Shoe Shop. I am sure that my first shoe-shine must have been a disaster with more polish on the man's socks than on his shoes, but I was a quick learner. Soon, I developed a system that created a shine to compete with the "spit-shine" that was standard with the marines who were stationed nearby at Camp Atterbury.

Camp Atterbury, in Columbus, Indiana, was a processing station for military personnel who were completing training and were destined to ship overseas soon. Many of them shipped to England and later went into combat in Germany. This was in 1942, and apparently, forces were being trained and assembled for the invasion of Europe. The young military men enjoyed weekend passes in Bloomington, and one of their rituals involved my shining their combat boots until they looked like glass. While I worked on their boots, they often made comments that indicated that they were well aware of the military action that lay before them. (I charged twenty-five cents for shining combat boots, but they often tipped me as much as a dollar.)

World War II was a frightening, gloomy, lonely time even for a ten-year-old boy. I was afraid my dad would be drafted, although he was almost too old and was married with six children. Almost all men of draft age were in the military, and already, some had been wounded or killed. (I heard of a young soldier who was killed in combat but had already written letters home. The dreaded telegram announcing his death arrived several days before his last letters. In a sense, he seemed alive until his last letter arrived.)

Metal products of every kind were in short supply, which meant that toys were very hard to find. Most Christmas toys were made of wood at home. Food, gasoline, tires, and clothing were rationed. New cars were not available, and used ones were scarce.

Everyone was encouraged to grow a "victory garden." IU Professor Robert Milisen turned the old Droll farm into fields of green beans, and all young boys (including myself) were encouraged to pick them at harvest time. The rows of beans were often about one-half mile long, and we usually picked down one row until noon and back that afternoon. We would crawl on our knees, dragging a basket with us and picking with both hands, rather like milking a cow. We were paid two and one-half cents per pound for picking, and we could earn approximately three dollars per day. I remember how hot it was and how sickening was the smell of jimson weeds under the sun. In the afternoon, we often took a break and went swimming in Getty's creek nearby. Since there were no girls present, we "skinny-dipped." After the swim, Dr. Milisen often appeared in his car with ice cream for all.

Perhaps the most frightening war experiences were the nightly blackouts when we were not allowed to have any lights, including fires. At these times, C-47 airplanes ("Gooney Birds") flew over our houses at low altitude, each towing two gliders. They were ghost-like, having no visible lights, but we could hear them and see their silhouettes against the moonlit clouds. Sometimes they were so numerous they seemed to fill the entire sky. Very likely, they were training for the invasion of Europe.

During summer vacations and on Saturdays during winter, I worked at the barbershop, riding to and from Bloomington with my father in his daily commute "back'erds and for'erds" to work. I developed considerable independence, being able to buy some of my clothing and other necessities as well as a few luxuries. The barbers, Pete and Richey, trusted me and gave me several new responsibilities, including deposits of cash to the bank just a few blocks from the barbershop. I began studying violin with Donald Neal, a graduate student at the IU School of Music. I rode the city bus to my lessons and paid for them out of my earnings. As I remember, lessons were one dollar at first, eventually rising to $1.25.

I owned two violins at that time. The first (six dollars) was an old red one that had belonged to a country fiddler and was in terrible condition. (I remember that the bridge was too low: it had been "improved" by placing pennies under each foot. It also had rattlesnake rattles inside, supposedly to improve the tone quality.) The second was a "conservatory violin," which I purchased from a lady who stopped me on the street when she saw me carrying my violin. Her husband had died several years earlier. The violin was his, and she had no use for it. It included a case, a bow, and an instruction book *EZ Method for Violin* (thirty-five cents). Until that time, I had *no* method for the violin, so the purchase price of four dollars for the outfit represented a real upgrade for me. I began studying the *EZ Method*, progressing from lesson to lesson as the book directed. After a few weeks of study, I came to the first tune in the book: *Aunt Dinah's Quilting Party.* I was playing it one night when my dad heard me practicing. He excitedly slammed the door open and ran into the room screaming, "That's a *tune*! You have to have private lessons!" So my lessons with Donald Neal began.

Donald Neal was well-known in Bloomington, having performed widely since high school. At that time, the IU School of Music was very small, contained completely in one building, which is still standing and still in use. The upper floor contained only practice rooms, and each student was assigned a practice room. Some students kept blankets and minimal "kitchens" in the practice rooms so they could live there.

Country fiddling was alive, well, and very active at that time. There was a saloon on Morton Street called the Bloody Bucket. I was never inside it, but I was told that it had a sawdust floor, at least one fight every night, frequent "killins" on weekends, and the loudest country fiddling to be found anywhere. A cheap, but very powerful, amplifier contributed to the volume. In the summer, when the windows and doors were open (no air-conditioning) the fiddle could be heard several blocks away. The fiddler used bass bow hair (black and very coarse), and wore it out every week so that his bow had to be rehaired every Saturday. I knew this because I began teaching violin at Rone's Music Store on Saturday mornings, and I saw the fiddler bringing his bow in for weekly rehairing.

The Bloody Bucket attracted members of the faculty at IU School of Music. I was told that on almost any night, one could find world-famous musicians dressed as local patrons sipping beer with the other customers and enjoying the fiddling.

Pete and Richey remained my friends for years, even after I graduated from IU, served in the Atlanta Symphony and the Air Force and came back to Bloomington for graduate work at IU. I often had them cut my hair, and we talked about old times. They scarcely believed what their former shoe-shine boy had experienced. I also had trouble believing it.

6

Our house on Getty's Creek Road was rather new, a Cape Cod on a flat lot with a creek running through it. The road was "pike"—that is, crushed stone (not asphalt). There was not much traffic on the road, but in the summer, any car would raise a monstrous cloud of dust as it passed. Fortunately, our house was set back from the road several hundred feet.

At age twelve, one of my chores was to take the cows to pasture each morning and return them to the barn lot in the late afternoon at milking time. This was a pleasant chore involving a half-mile walk in the woods by and through the creek. I often stopped to play in the creek after herding the cows into the pasture. There was shade from the sycamore trees, and in several places, the creek was deep enough for swimming. The bottom was mostly sandstone, and there were thousands of large geodes lying around. Geologists and their students often visited the area, loading their cars with samples of geodes to study. (They also tended to scare our horses and break down our fences, which did not endear them with my dad.) The water was crystal-clear and clean enough to drink. Our teachers in school taught us that when the ice age ended, the glacier stopped its southern progress near our community, depositing large amounts of stones from many northern locations.

One day, I saw a cloud of dust coming toward the house, but instead of continuing past the house, it turned into our driveway! I hurried home to find out what was happening. A stranger identified himself as a producer of television programs at the new television station in Bloomington, WTTV. He had heard that I played violin, and he invited me to play on TV. I immediately accepted his invitation and thus began a relationship with WTTS and WTTV (radio and television), which lasted until I began college about six years later.

The radio and television stations were a part of the Sarkes Tarzian Company in Bloomington. In addition to broadcasting, Mr. Tarzian operated a factory on the premises. The factory produced selenium rectifiers, an invention of Mr. Tarzian. He also invented a new form of radio broadcasting called Hi-Fam (high-frequency amplitude modulation), different from FM (frequency modulation). Hi-Fam had several advantages, but one definite disadvantage: it could not be received on normal radios without an adapter. Mr. Tarzian hoped that Hi-Fam would be so popular that everyone would purchase an adapter, but this did not materialize.

I soon became a sort of staff violinist at WTTS-WTTV. I would hang around the station for hours several days per week, practicing on the violin and exploring the factory. There were no networks, and all programming was either alive or by transcription. When music was needed to fill time at the ends of programs, I would be asked to play, which I did. (I don't remember *what* I played, but I doubt that it was very listenable.) I had the run of the station and the factory, and I made friends with many of the people working there. I earned twenty-five dollars per week, which I thought was a great amount of money. (My violin outfit with instruction book cost four dollars.) I distinguished myself in one memorable way: I am the only person, so far as I know, whoever flushed a toilet on the air.

Our restroom was located just off the control room. One day, I finished in the restroom and carelessly opened the door as I flushed. This was synchronized perfectly with the announcer giving a station break in the most dignified voice he could manage: "You are listening to WTTS, the friendly voice of...*KLO-O-S-SH-H!*"

We had heard quite a lot about television before it actually came to Bloomington. We knew that Mr. Tarzian planned to begin broadcasting TV in addition to radio, but we had not yet seen TV. Eventually, the furniture stores in Bloomington each received one TV set, which they installed in their windows. They placed speakers outside the windows so that people could watch TV after store hours (there were no broadcasts during the day at first, only test patterns, blue and white). People would bring chairs and sit on the sidewalk in front of the store windows, watching the test pattern until the evening broadcast began.

The only station we could receive was WLW in Cincinnati, Ohio. It was so distant we received more "snow" than picture. Tom Mix (western) movies were very popular in those early days. Tom usually wore a very tall white hat. I often confused the hat with the snow-capped mountains that figured in the plot of the movies.

WTTS and WTTV shared one broadcast studio and a control room. The walls were covered with inverted egg cartons for sound-proofing, but when the whole room was painted a uniform color, it looked rather good. At first there was only radio (WTTS), but WTTV was soon to follow, sharing the same studio. In addition to the microphones and stands, there was one television camera, a huge monster with three or four lenses. (Zoom lenses had not yet been invented.) There was no air-conditioning, so temperatures were very hot. There was also very little space, which resulted in frequent traffic jams in the studio during programs. Mr. Glen van Horn, a teacher at nearby Bloomington High School, served as advisor and facilitator for the stations, training announcers and supervising broadcasts. Several high school students became career broadcasters after working at WTTS-WTTV, including Jack Noel, Bob Hardy, and others. One of the singers, "Bouncin' Bobby Helms" recorded several hit records in Nashville, Tennessee, including "Fraulein," "My Special Angel," "Rockin' Round the Christmas Tree," and "Jingle Bell Rock."

I was invited to play on two thirty-minute programs that broadcast back-to-back once each week. They were *Uncle Bob Hardy and The Happy Valley Folks* and *The WTTV Golden Strings*. Both were broadcast live, and I had to change costumes during the station break. I believe I was the only person who played on both programs. *Happy Valley Folks* was a country music show; and *Golden Strings* was a string ensemble with piano playing waltzes, light classics, and Broadway show music. Performers in the *Golden Strings* were mostly students of Donald Neal, a well-known violinist/teacher who was a graduate violin student at Indiana University when I studied with him. Being a member of these two groups, I was often engaged to play at the Indiana State Fair, Monroe County Fair, weddings, etc. In retrospect, I have often been amazed at the amount of musical talent available in southern Indiana when I was young. Perhaps others who were in positions to develop this talent also recognized this. Indiana University School of Music began rapid expansion while I was in high school.

7

Students and teachers at Unionville High School warned me not to enroll at Indiana University. No student from Unionville had graduated from IU, although several had gone there to train as teachers. (At that time, teachers could be licensed with only two years of college after graduating high school.)

IU is a land-grant university. In 1950, when I enrolled, all graduates of accredited Indiana high schools were allowed to enroll at the university. No promises were made that we could remain there, however, and many students were dismissed by Thanksgiving. We had what we called "smoke-ups," pink slips warning if we were doing unsatisfactory work in any course. There was a limit upon the number of smoke-ups we could receive and still remain enrolled at the university.

Another advantage of a land-grant university was that tuition was essentially free for Indiana residents. There were a few fees to be paid, however, and when I enrolled, I usually received a bill for about thirty-five dollars per semester. Adding books and other necessities brought my costs to about 150 dollars per semester, to which I had to add living expenses. Since I could live at home, living expenses were very low, so I could work my way through college. I had a job at The Nurre Companies, makers of plate-glass mirrors. My responsibility was to run a small print shop, printing office forms and brochures for the seven plants that made up the company. I also ran the Addressograph, a machine that addressed direct mailings of advertising materials. I was allowed to set my own schedule, but I had to work forty hours per week. I can't remember exactly how much I was paid, but I am sure it was less than two dollars per hour.

I was a violin major at IU School of Music, a student of Urico Rossi, first violinist of the Berkshire String Quartet in Residence at the school. Upon the advice of Mr. Rossi, I was enrolled in both bachelor of music in violin and bachelor of music education with violin concentration. The two degrees were similar enough that I could complete both of them in five years rather than just one in four years. This, however, required a very heavy schedule in school in addition to forty hours per week at The Nurre Companies. For the first time in my life, I had to strictly budget my time, allowing five hours per night for sleep during the week, ten hours on Saturday, and fifteen on Sunday.

Majoring in violin required endless practicing, a minimum of four hours daily in addition to violin and chamber music lessons and two hours per day in orchestra rehearsals. I discovered that I could start the printing machine (called a multilith) with about one thousand sheets of paper and monitor it while practicing on the violin. This worked very well until I overlooked a problem one night and printed 2,600 brochures with a major defect in the company logo. The problem was in the "blanket" of the lithograph machine: blankets could develop low spots that could be corrected by replacing them with new blankets or by placing torn scraps of paper under the low spots. I didn't see the defect, so I did neither. The result was a large stack of expensive egg-shell bond paper rendered useless by my carelessness. I believe my boss must have been very sympathetic to my situation: I still had a job after the mistake was discovered.

The CEO of The Nurre Company in Bloomington was Mr. Distelhorst. He was a kindly man, always friendly with me on the rare occasions when I met him. He was the author of several form letters, which I printed and mailed out to a list of contacts whose names and addresses were on metal plates that ran through the Addressograph. The plates were filed in drawers that loaded into the Addressograph. It was my responsibility to keep the plates up to date by making replacements for outdated ones. The form letters were reproduced on metal plates that were attached to a metal drum on the multilith machine. The metal plates lasted a long time, but eventually, they wore out and had to be replaced. My responsibilities included ordering replacement plates through our office manager, Mr. Cates.

I was in the middle of my freshman year when one of the plates wore out. I had been placed in the second year of English Composition at Indiana University, based upon tests taken during orientation. I was quite proud of that placement, and I allowed my new knowledge of English composition to influence my judgment in ordering a new plate. I took a copy of the form letter and marked it in the manner my English Composition professor used in marking my papers. Since there were numerous errors in grammar, syntax, and punctuation in the form letter, it was considerably marked up when I sent it along with a purchase requisition to Mr. Cates!

It was necessary for Mr. Distelhorst to make changes to his letter before ordering a new plate. He made the suggested changes, however, and in a few days, I received a new plate along with a rather frosty note from Mr. Distelhorst in which he expressed the hope that the letter would be satisfactory. I heard the rumor that my letter and requisition had been widely circulated among the office staff, providing them with some much-needed humor.

Most of my work at the Nurre Companies was done after dark. I was usually the only person working except the night watchman, who made his rounds every hour using keys to record his visits to designated locations. The spooky old brick building had large windows, which probably had never had blinds and perhaps had never been washed. The ancient wood floors were rotten in places, and there were holes where the unwary could fall through. Impossibly large rats roamed everywhere: I could see their shadowy forms and glowing eyes when I walked through the building to the water fountain. Ancient machinery crowded the working area where during the day skilled workmen carved and sand-blasted beautiful designs in the finest plate-glass mirrors. The mirrors were treasured by wealthy homeowners in the days before modern methods and equipment were invented. The print shop was located in a room which in earlier times had housed the office and administrative staff, who had been moved to a separate suite of offices downtown in Bloomington. The room was well lighted, which meant that any person wandering in the alley could see me as I worked. Since the factory was near Morton Street, the red-light district of Bloomington and the location of several notorious taverns, I often suspected that I was being watched as I worked. I can remember times when I could almost feel the gaze of people outside: I wondered whether they might have some unpleasant plans for me.

Parked near the door of the print shop was my car, a black 1934 Buick Special in which I took great pride. It had belonged to an old man who didn't drive it for years, and when he died, the car was for sale as a part of his estate. It was like new, but the engine was frozen from non-use. I bought it for 275 dollars.

My uncle Lewis was a mechanic at Curry Buick in Bloomington, and he overhauled the engine for me at the cost of four hundred dollars. Most of my relatives thought I had invested too much in the car, but I drove it for several years with no trouble until the speedometer showed almost one hundred thousand miles. It was very handsome, in the style of the gangster cars shown in many movies. Girls seemed to enjoy riding in it.

When I finished my work, near midnight most nights, I walked about fifty yards in the dark alley to my parking place. Only a few bare bulbs lighted the area, and I was glad to get into my car and lock the door, preparing to go home.

I enjoyed working in the print shop. There was something magical in the transformation of blank paper into flyers, office forms, form letters, and posters. The process of lithography was fascinating to me, as my previous experience included only set type and printer's ink rolled onto the type. The work contrasted greatly with my efforts as a violin major at Indiana University, and I had to be able to transform from one personality to the other instantly every day.

I arrived at the music school every morning at about seven-thirty. Parking was a problem, and I often had to drive at least one-half mile before finding a parking place for the day. I didn't finish at school until about 5:30 p.m., and often, I had to return to the school in about one hour for special rehearsals or recital attendance. (Music majors were required to attend at least fifteen recitals each semester or lose three-fourths of an hour of general credit.) One night I encountered an unusual problem.

The recital ended at about 10:00 p.m., and I had to go to the print shop for several hours' work. By that time all the cars were gone near the music school, and I walked about a half-mile to my parked Buick, which was isolated by that time. As I approached my car, a policeman appeared out of the dark and stopped me. He asked me to account for my activities for the afternoon and evening of that day, which I was easily able to do. He seemed satisfied with my account and allowed me to leave to go to work. I found out later that someone had called the police after seeing a peeping tom in the neighborhood. The police had "staked out" my car, probably thinking it looked like the sort of vehicle such a person would use.

Music students often ate lunch at Brummett's Pharmacy across Third Street from the Music Building. We were always rushed, and the pharmacy was usually crowded. We generally ate a cheeseburger with fries and a chocolate milkshake, all of world-class quality as I recall. Students and faculty were jumbled together, some eating at the soda fountain while others waited impatiently, often standing crowded just behind the seated patrons. Some very famous concert artists would be standing over unknown students at the daily feeding time.

One day, I was seated at the soda fountain, waiting for the lunch I had just ordered. Madame Dorothea Manski, a famous Metropolitan Opera star, came in and stood just behind me. She was a well-known character on the campus, in addition to being a fabulous singer/teacher. (Madame Manski stories abound on the IU campus.) She was shaped like a caricature of a Wagnerian soprano, with formidable frontal and rear development. I felt as though I was sitting under a large shade tree. As my cheeseburger, fries, and shake were delivered to me, Madame Manski said in her heavy German accent, "Dot looks gute!" I didn't know whether to offer her a bite or the whole lunch.

All sophomore music majors were required to take Introduction to Music Literature, taught by Dr. Ralph Daniel. The course was intended to teach music history in an outline form, identifying major developments in musical style from antiquity to the twentieth century. Dr. Daniel lectured in class, and students spent many hours in the library, listening to assigned works on LP recordings. We learned to identify any part of the assignment so that we could name title, movement or section, and composer by hearing several seconds of the recorded selection in tests. (We called this "drop the needle.") Dr. Daniel analyzed the style of each composer with the students in class so that we could give a description of a particular style upon request.

One day, I was requested to describe the style of Brahms, which I felt confident to do. I compared Brahms to Beethoven, including types of works and general style. A good part of my description was a recitation of portions of Dr. Daniel's lectures. I made a slight error, though: Dr. Daniel had described Brahms's orchestral style as "turbid" (muddy). I said "turgid" (sexually aroused). This seemed to amuse Dr. Daniel greatly: in fact, it was something of a "show stopper" (class stopper?). After the laughter died away, Dr. Daniel said, "Well, I guess you could call it turgid."

Dean Wilfred C. Bain believed that music students should be comparable to apprentices learning music by studying and performing it. He also believed that the music faculty should be exemplary performers, leading such ensembles as the IU Philharmonic and performing as soloists in the IU community and in professional concerts throughout the world. Pursuant to this belief, the IU Philharmonic (of which I was a member) made several tours each year.

We would travel in large buses for about two weeks each tour, performing as many as three concerts each day. There was no time for individual practice, and we played the same program every concert. Often, we traveled with a chorus of as many as three hundred singers (the Philharmonic had about one hundred instrumentalists), which created a huge logistic problem. We wore the same tuxedos every day for the duration of the tour, which meant that we felt rather grungy after two weeks. (We commonly joked that our tuxedos would stand by themselves with no need to hang them up at night.) Our diet, provided usually by community-minded local groups, was almost the same every day. Sometimes we had the same diet for lunch and dinner: chicken, mashed potatoes, peas, bread, cherry pie, and coffee or milk. Our sleeping arrangements were in private homes. We would be assigned in groups according to the space available, and generally, we would share beds in pairs. This may have led to complications, but I never heard of them.

I remember particularly the tour when we performed *Belshazzar's Feast* by William Walton. We had played this long, difficult work many times. I was a sophomore, and my position was principal second violin (leader of the section). One of our concerts was quite memorable.

We played in an old motion picture theatre in southern Indiana. Apparently, the theater had been closed and unused for many years. It looked like a vaudeville house, with heavy red velvet curtains and ancient light switches. Dust hang in handful-sized clumps everywhere backstage, ready to fall at the slightest provocation. All painted surfaces were pea-green, partially peeled away and very soiled with ancient handprints, dents, and scratches. The entire back of the stage could be opened for access to the loading platform for ease in assembling scenery.

The stage was too small for our huge ensemble, and the orchestra pit was so small as to be useless in its original form. Someone apparently decided to remedy this by laying green oak planks across the pit and seating the string section of the orchestra on that improvised platform. This seemed promising except for one detail: Dean Bain (who was conducting) was a rather heavy man who included something like deep-knee bends in his conducting technique. This motion was continuous, in rhythm with the music. After a few minutes, the entire oak platform was moving in a sort of lope, making music-reading difficult for the orchestra. Clumps of dust, turned loose from their years of captivity, floated majestically in the air.

Dean Bain had one other habit that I found objectionable: he mouthed the words of the chorus in an effort to make diction clear. Unfortunately for me, the consonants caused him to spit almost continuously, and my position as principal second violin made me the most vulnerable target in the entire orchestra. I thought fleetingly about having an umbrella to shelter me, similar to the little red umbrella in the familiar insurance commercial, but that might have been a distraction for the audience. In spite of the loping and the spitting, I did my best, but I won't vouch for my performance that night.

There is a saying, "Harpists spend half their life tuning, and the other half playing out of tune." Not for a moment will I agree with this saying, but it does illustrate the difficulty of having a harp ready to play in tune when needed. About halfway through our performance, some eager stagehand opened the doors to the loading dock behind the stage. Immediately, a blast of cold Hoosier winter air swept into the theater with several disastrous results. The most noticeable result was that the harp instantly went out of tune, introducing pitch relationships theretofore unknown to human experience.

"Babylon was a gre-e-e-a-a-ate city!"

8

Walter Robert was a successful young concert pianist in his native Germany until the Nazis came into power. Like many other artists and intellectuals, particularly those of Jewish heritage, he had to leave Germany to avoid the horrors of concentration camp. Eventually, he made his way to Indiana University, where he was a highly regarded professor of piano. He was often characterized as a "walking encyclopedia": it was rumored that he could speak fourteen languages and that he could write seven of them fluently. He was the first musician I met who had recorded for a major label (RCA in his case). He was also the first pianist I ever heard who made the piano sound like a musical instrument.

Before enrolling at Indiana University, I had not knowingly met any Jews. In our community, we thought of Jews as people in the Old Testament. They had existed many years ago far away in Israel, which itself no longer existed. One day in orchestra, I met a community member (Rose Fell) whom our family had known well, but at first, I didn't recognize her in that surrounding. I discovered that she and her family were Jewish, and that there was a rather large community of Jewish people in Bloomington. Walter Robert was one of them.

In my third year of college, I took a course called *Form and Analysis*. The professor was Walter Robert. It was a challenging course that built upon the foundation of music theory, showing how the fundamentals of music shape large musical forms. We analyzed sections of large works, and we synthesized (composed) works in similar musical styles.

Following *Form and Analysis* I had *English Literature* in the building next to the music building. I had only ten minutes between classes, so I had to run from one to the other across tree plots (not taking the time to go around the walkways). As I ran the first day, I saw Mr. Robert running beside me. I asked him where he was going, and he answered that he was teaching a class next door. I was quite surprised when we both arrived at the same classroom. He was also my *English Literature* professor!

Our reading list for *English Literature* included the King James Version of *The Gospel According to Saint John* (chapter 1) along with a representative list of other masterworks. Mr. Robert introduced the *Gospel* by telling us about ancient Greek philosophers who believed that there was one basic principle that explained even the most complex things. (A modern example is the widely-known equation $E=mc2$ discovered by the famous violinist Albert Einstein.) Mr. Robert pointed out that the *logos* in the first chapter of John's *Gospel* is not completely translated as "word," but actually means "rational divine intelligence" related to "logic." It also contains the meaning *human reasoning reconciled with universal intelligence.* It couldn't mean "the Bible" as my community generally believed. The New Testament could not refer to itself, since it didn't exist until it was written and compiled. People who believe in Jesus believe that *logos* refers to Him. This was a life-changing revelation to me. It has informed much of my adult spiritual growth.

The famous $E=mc2$ has been extended in many ways during my lifetime. One way is the controversial "big bang theory." Perhaps this theory could be summarized: the universe expands and contracts in a sort of rhythm as it freely changes from matter to energy and back to matter. It is interesting to compare this theory with the Creation Story in Genesis. (Science does not contradict theology. Both represent efforts of humans to discover and express eternal truth. "E" has *always* equaled "mc squared." Is it unreasonable to believe that some part of this was understood by ancient Egyptians, Greeks, Jews, or Mayans?)

All the energy we have on earth is derived from nuclear energy, mostly from our sun. A negligible amount may come from other celestial sources, such as starlight. Petroleum was derived from the sun originally, and its energy has been stored underground until humans learned to pump it, refine it, and burn it in a variety of ways. All other forms of energy can be similarly traced to their beginnings as solar (nuclear) radiation. Harnessing any form of energy is always a dangerous undertaking, and we must balance the dangers with the advantages as a matter of stewardship.

It is rather surprising to me that many of our contemporaries believe that human beings should stop using nuclear power because of the inherent dangers of such use. We might join together in wishing nuclear power had never been discovered, but there is little reason to hope that this wish will be granted. It is easy to forget that many countries in the world have owned stockpiles of nuclear weapons for generations and that these weapons have been handled regularly by thousands of ordinary military personnel with no known accidental nuclear detonations. It seems reasonable to believe that with similar training and precautions the same standard of safety could be realized in peaceful uses of nuclear energy.

I have developed many personal opinions as an adult, and I have come to regard them as confessions. It is as though I am saying, "This is what I believe, so help me God." So to speak, "Here I raise my *Ebenezer*: hither by thy help I've come" (from the hymn "Come, Thou Fount of Every Blessing"). An extended opinion might take the form of my translation of the first few verses of the *Gospel of St. John*:

> Even if there is nothing material, the Mind of God exists. It is with God, and is the same as God. From the beginning of creation it is present, and it makes everything that is created."
>
> Creation takes place in eternity. Time does not exist at creation, since time is a product of the observation of motion of heavenly bodies, which did not exist until energy was transformed into matter. In eternity there is no past or future, only present. It is nearly impossible for human

beings to think in eternal terms since our lives are almost completely temporal. The Mind of God, however, is eternal. Apparently the history of humanity is contained in human efforts to connect with God. Apparently, also, God eternally seeks to reconcile with humanity. Human achievements seem to form links to eternity, that is, connections to God. Perhaps this is the source of paradox (seeming self-contradiction), which is at the very core of creation. How could expanding infinite space be filled with energy?

I believe that the Creator of humanity and the temporal universe is able to create eternal beings in infinity, which recognizes time and space but is not limited by them. From our earliest history to present time, we have hints of the nature of eternal life as "seen in a glass, darkly." These hints are preserved in the literature and artifacts of many cultures, and they are surprisingly similar. I believe that the Holy Bible, Old and New Testaments, is our richest source of intimations of eternity. They are presented as seen by the writers and in their vocabulary: our task is to translate them into expressions of eternity. Perhaps this is the reason for the account of the Day of Pentecost (New Testament Acts 2:1).

The poet Mary Frye has written:

I Did Not Die.

Do not stand at my grave and weep.
I am not there. I do not sleep.
I am a thousand winds that blow;
I am the diamond glints on snow.
I am the sunlight on ripened grain;
I am the gentle Autumn's rain.
When you awaken in the morning's hush
I am the swift uplifting rush
Of quiet birds in circled flight.

I am the soft star that shines at night.
Do not stand at my grave and cry.
I am not there;
I did not die.

I believe that the miracles described in the Bible are events reported by the people who witnessed and interpreted them according to human experience as miracles, but they were not miracles to the performers. The Creator is not limited in the *manner* of actions. When God said, "Let there be light," we are not informed about the time or space involved. "There was light" as an eternal expression. What was impossible in human (temporal) terms apparently was effortless eternally (easy to perform, difficult to explain).

Mr. Robert's course reshaped my spiritual development and introduced me to a much broader cultural experience than I expected. Chaucer's *Canterbury Tales* were also on the reading list. Until that time, I had no idea that such literature existed. I was immediately enthralled by it.

Early in the course, Mr. Robert read from *The Miller's Tale* in the early English version. It was rather tough going for me, except that some of the early English sounded much like the conversation I had heard in our community as I was growing up. (One of my high school teachers told our class that in the early 1930s, in the mountains of Tennessee, communities had been discovered that were practically identical with Elizabethan communities. My ancestors originated in that area.) Mr. Robert came to a verse that I found shocking: "Now Nickolas had risen for a piss!" Did an IU professor know that word? If he did, he must know the Other Two (even worse) words! (This was long before Dr. Kinsey did his research that resulted in the sensational publication *Sexual Behavior in the Human Male*.)

I didn't have more courses with Mr. Robert, but we continued to talk together when we had opportunities. We would often meet in Brummett's Pharmacy for a cup of coffee between classes. One day, Mr. Robert seemed depressed (a surprise to me: could an IU faculty member ever be *depressed*?). He talked about his youth in Germany, lamenting the fact that his homeland was gone forever. He also said that he felt that he had no home, even though he had been welcomed to the United States and was quite successful here. I mentioned how satisfying it must be to have so many talented students and to know that he had had an important influence upon them. He answered that many of his students expected unreasonable success in music and were heartbroken when they couldn't achieve such success. At that time, I had "success" only in the sense that I had been allowed to remain enrolled at Indiana University and that it appeared likely that I would be allowed to graduate. I said that I kept going because of my faith in God, and I asked him if he believed in God. I will never forget his answer: "I would like to believe, but I can't."

9

In my retirement home, my collection of music is stored in several rooms of the house and garage. In the teaching/recording studio, there is an old music cabinet with sliding shelves. This cabinet is used to store concertos, sonatas, and suites for violin and piano.

On the second shelf of concertos, just under the Bach and Beethoven works, is the *Brahmps Violin Concerto*, as pronounced by one of my teachers, Berl Senofsky.

At first, I wondered why he pronounced it that way. Then I reasoned that he tended toward rather dyspeptic speech, possibly because he became something of a *gourmand* in his later years. His rather generous girth and his attacks of gout were also possible results of his dietary habits, and he tended to refer to food in his teaching. I remember one case in point: I was invited to sit in on a lesson with violist Kim Kashkashian, a beautiful and gifted young lady. Mr. Senofsky brilliantly analyzed and illustrated one of the Brahms viola sonatas and coached Ms. Kashkashian in its performance. During the lesson, Mr. Senofsky remarked about the Brahms, "I take nourishment from it."

I experimented with the pronouncement of "Brahms" and discovered that if I kept my lips closed until the "m" sound and puffed a bit of air at that time it became "Brahmps"!

My copy of the Brahms *Concerto in D*, opus 77, Schirmer Edition, was edited by Efrem Zimbalist (yes, the father of the famous actor). I have owned this piece of music since 1954, and it is worn and covered with finger prints. The pages are no longer fastened together, although there are two very rusty staples through the middle pages, reminders of times long past. Practically every page, including the cover, could be framed as a work of art. The edges are worn in intricate patterns, and the paper is so fragile it crumbles often as pages are turned. At the top of the front cover is my name as I printed it when I was in college.

I had played the Bruch g Minor Concerto on my junior recital at Indiana University. My teacher, Urico Rossi, had patiently and carefully taught the Bruch to me, and the performance was quite successful. I was amazed when a few days later he asked if I would like to play the Brahms on my senior recital. No other IU undergraduate student at that time had performed the entire Brahms Concerto by memory in public. I felt totally inadequate to do so, especially since violinists generally felt that the Brahms should be undertaken only by very mature musicians. Yet I realized that such an opportunity was unlikely to occur again for me. When would I ever have the time to study this difficult work after I graduated? Prayerfully and with great trepidation, I accepted the assignment. Thus began a lifetime studying this great masterpiece.

The Brahms is really a symphony concertante—that is, a symphony with a very important solo part. It is extremely difficult, but not virtuosic in the usual sense. It demands the highest level of technical and musical ability. It begins with an extended exposition by the orchestra, joined at times by the soloist as a bow to the tradition of earlier concertos, which were played with the principal violinist of the orchestra as soloist.

The first solo entrance is a sort of accompanied cadenza, which introduces the main theme. I was amazed that Mr. Rossi could play this piece, illustrating it and editing my new music. Actually, he had done the same thing with the Bruch Concerto and with other impressive pieces, but somehow, the Brahms was different. I have since studied it with other teachers, and some of Mr. Rossi's editing has been changed, but most of the markings in my copy are his, dating from 1954.

Each well-worn page evokes memories that I thought were forgotten. The first solo entrance recalls different experiences, separated by several years…

Shortly after I began studying the Brahms I, along with several other students and faculty members, was invited to rehearse and perform a concert with the Evansville (Indiana) Philharmonic. The talented young conductor Minos Christian was to conduct with the famous Hungarian virtuoso violinist Joseph Szigeti performing the Brahms Concerto. In those days, orchestra players often quoted the maxim "Conductors use batons of a length inversely proportional to their ability." The inexperienced Mr. Christian used a very long baton.

The orchestra had three hours to rehearse the entire program, which included an overture, the concerto, and another symphonic composition. Mr. Szigeti more or less took charge of the rehearsal during the Brahms, leaving Mr. Christian rather helpless. Mr. Szigeti stormed up and down the stage, criticizing (insulting) individual performers and generally expressing dissatisfaction with the ensemble. Predictably, the orchestra lost confidence and became very tired.

At the concert, the overture went rather well. The orchestral exposition of the Brahms also was quite acceptable. Then Mr. Szigeti began the solo entrance with a rather harsh, aggressive style. On the thirteenth bar, where the slurred arpeggios begin, he somehow allowed the tip of his bow to slip between the two top strings. It was stuck there for what seemed a long time, and the sound was (in the words of Hoosier fiddlers) "like cats a-fightin." Generally, orchestra players are sympathetic to soloists, probably because most orchestra members have experience performing the solo part and know the perils thereof. In this case, there was little sympathy. I heard at least one person (perhaps myself) mutter, "It couldn't happen to a better person."

During the summer of 1954, Mr. Tossy Spivakovski was visiting professor of violin at IU. My teacher, Mr. Rossi, was first violinist of the Berkshire Quartet in residence at Music Mountain, Connecticut. Since he couldn't be at Indiana that summer, I wanted to study with Mr. Spivakovski.

I went to my first scheduled lesson with Mr. Spivakovski, hoping to get some pointers that would be useful in my preparation of the Brahms Concerto. I already knew that Mr. Spivakovski had developed a unique technical approach to violin playing since my first teacher, Donald Neal, had studied with him for several years. I couldn't consider changing my entire technique during that summer, so I hoped to get as much help as possible using my rather standardized technique.

When Mr. Spivakovski began playing the Brahms first solo entrance, it was a revelation to me. He used different fingerings from those in my edition, and his technique was as different from traditional technique as it could be. In addition, the playing was absolutely clean, in tune, and easy. I wanted to be able to continue studying with Mr. Spivakovski, but it wasn't possible. However, he did change some of the editing of my copy. He also recommended that I go to San Francisco, California, and study with Naom Blinder, the teacher of Isaac Stern. In my circumstances, this was almost the equivalent of suggesting that I go to the moon. Mr. Spivakovsky made some other notations in my Brahms copy, among them an explanation of the difference between chromatic and diatonic half-steps. This led to a discussion of the Pythagorean *comma*, which led to a discussion of different tuning systems.

Thirty-three measures before letter "G" in the first movement is a very difficult passage involving shifts primarily to intervals of descending and ascending major and minor ninths, a melodic expansion of a simple wavering chromatic line. I made this passage into an exercise, which included practically every shift available on the violin. I practiced this exercise every day, regardless of the effect it may have had on every person, dog, or cat in the vicinity. One person reacted verbally to my practicing.

I had been invited to membership in the Fort Wayne (Indiana) Symphony, a paid position that would help with my expenses while living in Fort Wayne and doing my student teaching during the last half of my senior year (1955). Dr. Newell Long, faculty member in Music Education at IU, made the arrangement. I was delighted to have the opportunity: it was my first professional symphonic experience. I lived in the YMCA, a rather comfortable building similar to an inexpensive hotel with dining room. I needed a place to practice on the violin since practicing in my room was not allowed. I asked the manager if I might use the chapel since it was seldom occupied. Probably thinking that I would be playing music appropriate to worship, he gave me permission.

A few days later, the manager told me I would no longer be allowed to practice in the chapel. Someone passing by the door had heard me and objected to such misuse of the room. His exact words were "It sounded like a pig caught in a fence." I explained to the manager about the Brahms, and he rather hesitantly reinstated my practicing permission.

In 1955, the Fort Wayne Symphony was a very fine community orchestra that enjoyed great support from the community. Igor Buketoff was the conductor, and Hugo Gottesmann the concertmaster. I was placed in the first violin section, near the back. I felt quite anonymous there, and I didn't covet attention from anyone. I did, however, learn my orchestra parts thoroughly, never attending a rehearsal without being prepared. (I had been advised by my dear friend, Bonnie Bell, to always practice my orchestra music.)

Shortly after my arrival in Fort Wayne, I went to the first symphony rehearsal. We had just received music for our first concert, which included a new composition called *Sinfonietta Flamenca* by a contemporary composer named Surinach. The music was in handwritten manuscript, and it was quite difficult. I practiced it assiduously along with the rest of the program.

As the rehearsal began, I noticed that the assistant concertmaster was absent. Mr. Gottesmann stood to tune the orchestra, and I noticed him looking around among first violinists. He caught my eye and beckoned me to come up and sit next to him! I was shocked. I had no idea that he even knew of my existence, but I went up to the first stand. Fortunately, I had prepared the Surinach, the first composition to be rehearsed that night. I played it as well as anyone in the orchestra and received approval from Mr. Gottesmann and Mr. Buketoff. I was no longer anonymous!

My student teaching was done primarily at Central High School of Fort Wayne, a large inner-city school. The students and their families were mostly lower-class socioeconomically. The parents were generally unskilled laborers who worked long hours for little pay.

More than half of the students were white with the other half divided between African-American and Hispanic races. The students were very well-behaved and highly motivated, apparently viewing education as their primary means of social mobility. They were extremely handicapped by the lack of financial resources, many of them unable to afford school cafeteria lunches. I knew several teachers who invited at least one student to lunch every day. I quickly established a good relationship with my students, with mutual respect. I don't recall a single disciplinary problem with my classes, although I do remember a few snickers when I made the usual "student-teacher" gaffes.

The music program at Central was primarily band and chorus. The band director was untrained in string instruments, but he maintained a group of about twenty students who struggled to learn to play string instruments with little instruction. I was assigned to teach these students, and I immediately discovered that they knew practically nothing about their instruments. They seemed to appreciate my efforts, and we made excellent progress at the beginning level. Their prior performing experience consisted of playing in front of the band (forming a sort of orchestra in which the strings were inaudible). They seemed surprised and delighted to find that they could form an ensemble that could play music with just string instruments. It was also possible to play *specific pitches*!

The band was large, well-balanced instrumentally, and impressively skilled. I don't know how they managed to secure instruments of generally high quality, but they did. They seemed to instruct each other in sectional rehearsals before and after school and during lunch periods. Their director seemed to operate primarily as an organizer, but he was very effective. One of their concert performances was a very fine arrangement of Richard Strauss's *Till Eulenspiegel*.

The large, well-balanced chorus was equally impressive. They performed at least one concert while I was there (one semester), which included a good arrangement of *South Pacific*. I was assigned to conduct one short selection by band, chorus, and strings on the concert. The performances went well.

I was impressed by my student teaching experience at Central, particularly when combined with my experience in the Fort Wayne

Philharmonic. I learned to respect everyone associated with the school system as well as the Philharmonic, especially appreciating the spirit of cooperation that was evident in both organizations. I didn't think of working in such a situation at that time: I was preparing to graduate from IU and to serve in the United States Air Force. I also was resigned to the idea that I might not survive military service, so I didn't do much in preparation for subsequent life.

After student teaching, I returned to Bloomington to complete my work for the degrees bachelor of music education with violin concentration and bachelor of music with violin major (performance). The high point of this work was my senior recital, where I performed the Mozart *Sonata in B-flat, K. 454* and the complete Brahms *Concerto* (from memory). It was generally successful, though not as good as my rehearsals. Like all academic recitals, this one was recorded. I received a copy, which is actually an acetate recording that I have never been able to play. It seems that heat has melted and distorted the acetate. I still have it, though, hoping that I can find a way to play it. It is very difficult for a performer to remember a performance accurately. Usually, one can remember only the wrong notes!

I will always be grateful to Urico Rossi for suggesting the Brahms *Concerto* to me. I have had many experiences with it since my senior year. I still restudy it occasionally, finding to my surprise that I can play it better with each restudy. I don't have the stamina to play the whole composition, but I find great satisfaction in playing separate movements on subsequent days.

Some of my most enjoyable listening has included the Brahms *Concerto*. Geza de Kresz, violinist of the Royal Conservatory in Toronto, Canada, was a guest faculty member at IU one summer when I was studying there. He was a student of the great Eugene Ysaye, a founder of the Franco-Belgian School of Violin Playing. M. de Kresz was seventy-three years old at the time (eight years younger than I am now!) and no longer playing in public. He performed the Brahms *Concerto* (first movement) informally for his students and a few friends. It was a touchingly beautiful performance. Intonation was undependable, vibrato was shaky, and other technical problems were evident, but the style was there along with the years of devotion.

Many years later, I was awarded a medal by the Ysaye Foundation for my efforts in performing unaccompanied Ysaye in the Baltimore/ Washington area. Awarding the medal was Antoine Ysaye, the son of Eugene Ysaye, the teacher of M. de Kresz!

I followed the career of another great violinist, Isaac Stern, rather carefully. His career included many magnificent performances of the Brahms *Concerto*. I was present in the orchestra for two such performances, one with the Atlanta Symphony in 1955 and the other with the Nashville Symphony in approximately 1962. In both performances, Mr. Stern played with a rather aggressive approach, probably the result of playing with orchestras in conditions where the soloist had to struggle to be heard.

The last time I heard Mr. Stern play the Brahms was years later, following a period of time when he was busy promoting the restoration of Carnegie Hall in New York. He performed three concertos on television to celebrate his sixtieth birthday, ending with the Brahms. His playing seemed to have been transformed: he played the Brahms with exquisite sensitivity, almost like chamber music. I heard no wrong notes, no roughness, only sublime music-making befitting a resident of Mt. Olympus.

10

High Flight
Oh! I have slipped the surly bonds of Earth
And danced the skies on laughter-silvered wings;
Sunward I've climbed, and joined the tumbling
mirth
Of sun-split clouds,—and done a hundred things
You have not dreamed of—wheeled and soared
and swung
High in the sunlit silence. Hov'ring there,
I've chased the shouting wind along, and flung
My eager craft through footless halls of air...
Up, up the long, delirious blue
I've topped the wind-swept heights with easy grace
Where never lark, or ever eagle flew—
And, while with silent, lifting mind I've trod
The high untrespassed sanctity of space,
Put out my hand, and touched the face of God.

This poem, by John Gillespie Magee, Jr. was published in February 1942. The author, an American, had broken the law by crossing the border into Canada and volunteering to fight the Nazis when he was eighteen years old. Within a year, he was sent to England and assigned to 412 Fighter Squadron, RCAF where he flew the Supermarine Spitfire fighter plane. He sent the poem to his parents on the back of a letter describing a recent test flight in which he had climbed to 30,000 feet. Three months later, he was killed after his plane collided with a trainer over the village of Roxholm. A farmer testified that he saw the Spitfire pilot struggle to push back the canopy of his plane, finally standing up to jump at an altitude too low for his parachute to open. He died instantly, at age nineteen.

I don't remember when I first read this poem, but it could have been shortly after its publication, when I was ten years old. I had many interests, but flying was very high on the list along with violin playing. I can remember riding my bike several miles to the Monroe County Airport near Bloomington. I would stand outside the fence watching the small planes take off and land from the short sod strip. They were mostly Aeronca Champs, small two-seaters usually painted yellow with a large area of orange on the fuselage. I watched as they did their takeoff runs, magically transforming from earth-born machines to soaring miracles, then reversing the transformation as they landed. I could see the pilots as their planes broke ground, and I could sense that at that instant their world changed. *"Behold, all things are new!"* Someday I would do that!

Years later, when I studied and performed the Brahms *Violin Concerto* with Urico Rossi at Indiana University, I associated the poem *High Flight* with the Adagio movement of the *Concerto*. I would be interested to know whether the poet knew Brahms's *Concerto*, but I wouldn't be surprised if he did. I haven't tried to find an exact correspondence between poem and music, but there is at least some correspondence in broad outline. The lovely oboe solo at the beginning of the Adagio is simple, like a folk-song with primary harmonies, basic rhythms and predictable form. This melody could represent the *"surly bonds of earth"* (I question the word *surly*). I have never heard this oboe solo played badly!

Following the oboe solo, the solo violin "takes off" into a sublime set of variations, which combine classical principles with rhapsodic romantic freedom that tends to obscure the fact that the movement *is* a set of variations. Tonal relationships, melodic creation, instrumental exploitation, and rhythmic expansion explore the limits of possibility playfully in a manner that sounds easy. The body of the poem corresponds in mood to the violin solo, ending with a simple authentic perfect cadence *"Put out my hand, and touched the face of*

God." In my opinion, this movement has seldom been equaled and never surpassed in the history of music.

After graduating from IU and finishing pilot training, I was assigned to McConnell Air Force Base in Wichita, Kansas, to transition into the B47 flying in Strategic Air Command. This was a ninety-day program in lieu of Advanced Flight Training. Since it was a relatively short program, living conditions were rather spartan at McConnell. We lived in open-bay barracks, generally satisfactory since we spent hardly any time there except while sleeping. (There were no provisions for violin-practicing, and almost no time either!) Sunday afternoons were the exception, and on one such afternoon, I found myself alone in the barracks after attending church and having a good dinner. I had the overwhelming urge to practice on the violin and to play the *Adagio* from the Brahms *Concerto*! Since I was alone in the barracks, I took my violin out of its case and began. After a brief warm-up, I felt like playing the *Adagio*, which surprised me since my recent practicing had been minimal (read *zero*). I knew the psychological "explanation" for this: "spontaneous recovery" from my psychology class at IU. (It was more a description than an explanation.) Amazingly, I *did* play it well, and as I played, the barracks room gradually filled with fellow students coming back from lunch. I continued playing to the end of the movement (probably not more than five minutes for most of my friends). They seemed to enjoy my playing, probably the most unusual event ever to take place in that building!

Many millions of people have *heard* the Brahms Violin *Concerto* (a smaller number have *played* it). Many more millions have flown as *passengers* in a great variety of planes (fewer have flown as *pilots*). How many have done all four activities? Thanks to Urico Rossi and Mr. Robert Wildman (my first flight instructor) *I have*!

11

After the monumental first movement (which stretches motivic development almost to the breaking point) and the soaring *Adagio*, Brahms ends his violin concerto with a joyous romp reminiscent of his *Hungarian Dances*. While the movement abounds in soloistic fireworks, it never resorts to the empty showmanship of many concerto finales. The composer does not exploit the high range of the solo violin as much as do many other composers of the time, preferring the more mellow middle and low ranges. His brilliant orchestration serves to avoid the muddiness sometimes characteristic of the music of Robert Schumann: solo double-stops, chords, and arpeggiated melodies in these ranges test the abilities of great violins and violinists, but in the hands of appropriate soloists, these concerns seem to disappear.

One must remember that this concerto is written as a symphony with solo violin. The orchestra parts are challenging to professional players, ensemble-playing is difficult, and conducting requires great skill. (Wisely, this concerto is seldom attempted in public by amateur or community orchestras.) In spite of its difficulties, I have never heard a bad public performance of this movement. It almost seems that all performers are inspired to give of their best as a celebration of success if the first and second movements go well. I remember one performance where impending disaster was averted with aplomb.

While working on my doctorate at Catholic University, I was invited by one of my teachers, Miran Kojian, to attend a concert of the Washington National Symphony, where he was concertmaster.

Featured soloist was the great violinist Zino Francescatti performing the Brahms *Concerto*.

The entire concert went well, as expected. In the *Coda* of the last movement of the Brahms, after the second solo entrance (the triplet phrases) there is a brief three-measure rest for the soloist before the sixteenth-note climax begins. At the beginning of the rest, a string broke on Mr. Francescatti's Stradivarius. The audience could hear the breaking string, and an audible gasp arose. Mr. Francescatti quickly exchanged violins with Mr. Kojian, who passed the ailing violin to the violinist behind him, and the priceless instrument made a journey to the last stand violinist, each substituting his own instrument as he received the one with the broken string. The last violinist left the stage to replace the broken string from his stock of spares (all violinists carry spares). Mr. Francescatti made his entrance without missing a note, and the concert continued to a glorious end. The restrung violin was passed back to the soloist, who played an encore on it, receiving thunderous applause from an ecstatic audience. It was as though the broken-string episode had been carefully rehearsed!

After the concert, I spoke to Mr. Kojian, asking him why his violin sounded somewhat weaker than Mr. Francescatti's Strad. I knew that Mr. Kojian played one of the Stradivarius violins owned by the Smithsonian Institute. Mr. Kojian said that he wondered about this also and had asked Mr. Francescatti, who explained that he played somewhat more reservedly than usual because he was concerned about his intonation playing the strange instrument.

12

I met Teena (Elpha Ernestine) Patton in 1950 when she was sixteen years old. Her brother, Todd, worked at Nurre Companies when I began operating the print shop there just after graduating high school. Todd gave me a picture of Teena that was taken when she was fourteen, a very attractive "bobbysoxer." Later, he introduced me to her at their home when I stopped in for lemonade.

There was no immediate romance. I was a college freshman, and Teena was a lowly high-school student at University High, the laboratory school operated by IU. With my busy schedule, there was little time for dates, but I dated a few college girls on special occasions when couples only were invited.

Somehow, I knew that Teena and I would have a special relationship, but that would have to wait. I needed to complete the Air Force experience before I could have any permanent involvement leading to marriage. I also thought that there was a possibility that I would not survive pilot training. The military made that possibility quite clear in communications with prospective members. We were required to serve, and during that period of service, our lives were the property of the United States Government. The rationale for that arrangement was also stated: able-bodied young men owed military service to the nation in exchange for the protection our government provided to us and our families. This concept would be severely challenged a few years later when many young men replied, "Hell no! We won't go!"

During my third and fourth years at IU, I was a member of Advanced Air Force ROTC, the college training program for ir orce officers. This was during the Korean War, and I was deferred from the military draft until I could finish college and enter the Air Force as a second lieutenant. As we would joke later, I wanted to learn to fly in the worst way, so I entered the Air Force, and sure enough, it was the worst way! (This was purely a joke: Air Force pilot training was excellent. It was amazing that students such as I could take first demonstration flights in aircraft and graduate with wings in about one year.)

I was required to spend at least two years active duty in a chosen branch of the military (Universal Military Training). In order to be in pilot training, I had to commit to three years of active duty plus seven years reserve duty as a pilot. At my commencement, I received two degrees, my commission as an Air Force second lieutenant, and a letter from the Air Force saying that I would not be needed for *ten months* due to overcrowded flight school classes. I had planned to begin active duty immediately upon graduation. Suddenly, I needed a job!

RCA had a factory south of Bloomington, and they were in twenty-four hours-per-day operation. I was employed immediately after my application and assigned to the night shift. As I remember, my hours were 6:00 p.m. until 3:00 a.m. with one-hour break at 11:00 p.m. for lunch. I didn't complain about the schedule: I needed the money!

My work at RCA was on the assembly line making television sets. Television was relatively new and rapidly growing. We assembled two basic sets: one for table-top and one for stand-alone use (the "console" model). As I saw the sets, both were essentially the same with the difference that the console model had wires for two very cheap speakers. This was not stereo sound: both speakers received the same signal. The console model was hyped as a beautiful piece of furniture. It was in reality a very cheap, large (mostly empty), plywood box finished in a coat of hard lacquer that looked like glass. All hidden parts of the box were made of material much like cardboard. The tuning mechanism, which indicated channels, was so cheap and poorly designed that it often stopped working while it was on the assembly line! My job was to adjust the tension on a rubber belt so that the mechanism worked. The belt ran on two pulleys that were so flimsy they couldn't hold the belt in tension regardless of how well it was adjusted.

Each television chassis traveled on an overhead conveyor from one operator to another. The operator would place the chassis on a table, perform the operation, and return the chassis to the conveyor. Often, the chassis would fall off onto the concrete floor, and the operator would pick it up and sling it back as the conveyor moved to the next station. Any damage repair was left to quality control.

Workers on the assembly line were protected by a strong labor union, which meant that they almost could not be fired. Six workers near my station arranged to have one person perform six operations while the other five spent hours in the men's room shooting dice. One of the dice players would rotate to the assembly line every thirty minutes. When the foreman asked one of them (where I could over-hear the conversation) what he was doing, the answer was "I'm not doing anything, and I'm not going to do anything." Not surprisingly, before the summer was over, RCA had a huge warehouse full of tele-vision sets that no one wanted to buy. The result was closure of that plant and layoff of the workers, but I was not worried. *I had mine!* I was preparing to go to Atlanta, Georgia.

Earlier that summer, I was notified that the Atlanta Symphony was looking for violinists. The orchestra was described in glowing terms, including the facts that it was a professional, full-time orches-tra and that it was rated among the top ten professional orchestras in the United States. I was quick to accept all these claims and eager to audition, which I did. At that time, auditions could be done by tape recording, as I did mine. In a few days, I received word that I was invited to join the Atlanta Symphony in August. I checked the year's schedule and found that I was due at Lackland Air Force Base in San Antonio, Texas, three days after the end of the symphony season. I could make it! I immediately accepted the invitation and began to plan my move to Atlanta.

I had hardly been away from home before, my most extensive travel having been to Barksdale Air Force Base for ROTC summer camp the previous summer. That trip had been by Greyhound Bus, freeing me from any planning or driving. The trip to Atlanta was to be very different: I would be driving my 1950 Ford and actually *leaving home.*

I had traded for the Ford, thinking it would be dependable transportation: it turned out to be probably the worst car Ford ever made! It had belonged to a young lady who apparently had never heard of automobile maintenance. It had only twenty-six thousand miles on the speedometer, and the dark blue body was in generally good condition. However, it had a flat-head, six-cylinder in-line engine, made by a company that specialized in V-8s. One of its many weaknesses was that it wore out starter motors about every five thousand miles. That nasty habit caused grief for me on quite a few occasions, one of which (I realized much later) was actually quite humorous.

I bought a road map and planned my route using primarily Highway 41, the most direct route to Atlanta at that time. I was rather apprehensive about the adventure, but I had little choice. I packed my few belongings into the Ford, filled it with gasoline, slept through my last night at home, and left early one dewy late-summer morning. I was Atlanta-bound!

13

Southern Indiana is beautiful in late summer. In the early morning, everything is covered with dew so plentiful it could be rain. In the bright sunlight, the scenery appears magical, like an early Technicolor movie. White cumulous clouds float between the horizons almost as if an amateur artist had placed them. I had to wipe the windshield and windows of the Ford in order to drive safely, perhaps taking a bit longer than necessary: symbolically this was "goodbye" to the home of my youth.

I drove through Bloomington, every building and street reminding me of events I thought were forgotten. South on Walnut Street, past Pete and Richie's Barber Shop, past the jail and WTTS-WTTV, then out of town I went south toward Atlanta.

Oolitic, Bedford, Mitchell, Orleans, and Paoli were all familiar, part of my territory. I had been to New Albany and Louisville a few times, but they seemed foreign to me. The South began in New Albany, where for the first time, I saw water fountains and restrooms marked "Whites Only" or "Blacks Only." The "Blacks Only" facilities always seemed shabby, dirty, and crowded while those for "Whites Only" seemed completely adequate, clean, and almost deserted. I had scarcely heard of segregation at the time, probably because Unionville was lily-white, and Bloomington had only a few non-whites, mostly natives of foreign countries who were associated with Indiana University.

I continued through New Albany, across the Ohio River, through Louisville, and into Kentucky. My Ford was running well, and I was beginning to feel hungry. I stopped in a pretty little road-

FAR...BEYOND THE STARRY SKY

side park to eat the lunch Mom had packed for me. It was delicious, including the best fried chicken I had ever tasted, one of Mom's dinner rolls that almost floated in the air, and a large piece of apple pie with crust substantial enough to hold while eating but tender and flaky in the mouth. Apples, sugar, cinnamon, and magic combined to make that pie unforgettable. I don't know how I managed to swallow food past the lump in my throat. Tears clouded my eyes and ran down my cheeks as I remembered: I would visit home many times in the future, but never again would I live there! I tried to recall every unpleasant event in my experience, hoping to balance my sadness at leaving. It didn't work: there simply weren't enough such events.

Somewhere between Louisville and Chattanooga, I began to feel tired. As I recall, I was driving on Highway 41, which at the time was a two-lane, rather narrow highway that ran through every town, usually stopping at every traffic light. No one had thought of bypasses at that time. (Later, when I saw the movie *Bonnie and Clyde*, I recognized that the roads were similar.) I looked for a place to spend the night.

The word *motel* was not in general usage at that time. *Tourist cabins* or *tourist homes* were available. These were usually like small houses, rather new, in good condition, and generally attractive. Inside were one or two rooms, a lavatory, and a very small bath with tub and stool. There was one full-size bed, and smaller cots were available at extra cost. Sometimes a separating curtain on a wire could be drawn to separate the bedroom into two sleeping areas. There was a small porch on the front, furnished with a comfortable chair or porch swing. As I remember, the cost per night was less than five dollars. I found one of these beside the road and decided to stop there.

A young girl, perhaps eighteen years old, was working at the reception desk. I guessed that she was the daughter of the owner. She was attractive and friendly as she collected my money and arranged for my cabin. I drove up to the cabin, went in, and began preparing for the night. In a few minutes, the girl came in and began checking to see that everything was in order. I assumed that this was the usual practice, but she didn't leave when she had finished checking. She seemed to want to hang around, asking several times if she could do anything to make me more comfortable. Assuming that she meant changing something in the already-satisfactory room, I thanked her and said that nothing was needed. Much later, it occurred to me that she may have been offering herself! I was immensely flattered but confused. Nothing like this had happened to me before, and I had difficulty believing it could be possible. How could a total stranger take such an interest in me? I had always thought myself awkward, unattractive, and generally uninteresting. I also believed that any kind of sexual activity outside of marriage was sinful. (I was a baptized believer, *"Dead to trespasses and sin... It is no longer I: Christ liveth in me."*) I couldn't consider any relationship that might lead to marriage because I didn't expect to survive my military duty, and I didn't want to subject a young wife to a life of such uncertainty. The general attitude of my community was "Don't date a girl if you cannot imagine marrying her." I knew some people who had violated that rule, but I believed them to be in peril of the fires of hell. These attitudes would be seriously challenged very soon.

After a refreshing night's sleep, I continued toward Atlanta. Most of the pain of leaving home was gone, and I began to eagerly anticipate my new adventure. My dream of working full-time as a member of a professional symphony orchestra was about to become a reality! Fleetingly, I wished that it would be possible to stay in Atlanta permanently, but Universal Military Training denied that choice.

I arrived in Atlanta in midafternoon and found the symphony office without difficulty. It was on a narrow street, but I was able to park very near the front door. I was greeted by the manager, who introduced me to Mr. Henry Sopkin, the conductor. Both men were friendly and seemed to be concerned with my welfare. I noticed a sort of *knowing look* between them, and the manager picked up the telephone. After talking for a few minutes, he offered to introduce me to Mr. Rudolph Kratina, the recently-retired principal cellist of the symphony. Mr. Kratina had an extra room in his house that I could rent if I wished. I was immediately interested and accepted the offer of a room. I soon discovered that the opportunity to spend a season in the Kratina household would have made the entire venture in Atlanta worthwhile even if I disregarded any connection with the symphony!

The Kratinas lived in a comfortable two-story house in Ansley Park, a historic section of north Atlanta. Within walking distance was a fine Greek restaurant where I could eat most meals. (I walked past the filling station where Margaret Mitchell, authoress of *Gone with the Wind* was hit by an automobile, resulting in her death.) I usually ate a light breakfast at the Kratina's and had lunch and dinner at the restaurant (Rhodes Restaurant), owned by Gus Spiliotis. The food was very good, and the prices seem miniscule compared with those of today. I could have lunch *and* dinner for less than five dollars!

Mr. Spiliotis and I became good friends almost as soon as he found out that I was a violinist in the symphony. He had come to New York from Greece when he was twelve years old, sent by his father who was so poor that he could not support him. He arrived in New York with only the clothes he was wearing, met his older brother who owned a restaurant, and began working there. After learning the restaurant business, he was able to purchase Rhodes Restaurant. He was married to a beautiful young lady, and they had a lovely daughter about eight years old. Mr. Spiliotis had studied violin about one year in Greece. He wanted me to teach him, which I was delighted to do!

Violin lessons with Mr. Spiliotis were usually on Saturday mornings at about ten o'clock. We fell into a pattern: I would arrive at about 9:00 a.m., and Mrs. Spiliotis would serve a sumptuous breakfast for the family (including me). Included was something new to me: hot tea with honey, served in a tall glass with a long spoon for stirring. Breakfast lasted about one hour, followed by violin study for about two hours, followed by lunch (another sumptuous meal), then more violin study as time and energy permitted. Mr. Spiliotis made excellent progress from a review of beginning technique through the Handel *F Major Sonata*. He would simply walk out of his restaurant when lesson time came, leaving it to the care of his staff! He had spent many years wishing to study violin, and when the opportunity came, he embraced it with enthusiasm.

Atlanta had many fine eating establishments in addition to Rhodes Restaurant. There was a tiny *Bistro* that seated about twenty patrons and that featured authentic *coq au vin* for lunch at a cost of about five dollars. The chef was also the owner and waiter. Among many other excellent restaurants of various national origins one that must be mentioned was Leb's Delicatessen, a rather large room with a varied menu from which I usually chose blintzes with sour cream or the large dinner salad priced at about two dollars. Most of the members of the symphony would meet at Leb's after concerts to share a meal and revel in the success of the evening. Both orchestra and community shared great enthusiasm for music. (I often saw a rabbi shake hands with a musician and slip a ten-dollar bill into his pocket.) We felt fortunate that we were able to communicate in the medium and, in spirit, engage in musical conversations with the represented composers.

For some reason, I was downtown late one night. I was ravenously hungry and looking for a restaurant. I spotted one that was still open for business. On the window, it said *kosher*, a word I had seen before but didn't know the meaning. I thought it would be fine for my needs, so I went in and was seated. The waitress arrived to take my order: a cheeseburger with French fries and a chocolate shake. (I couldn't go wrong: that was my default meal throughout college.) The shocked waitress said, "I can't serve that here!"

"Why not?" I answered.

She replied, "Thou shalt not boil a kid in its mother's milk."

Kid? Mother's milk? Mystified, I ordered another favorite, blintzes with sour cream *and* applesauce. A few years later, I learned the meaning of *dairy* versus *deli*!

Mr. Kratina (Rudolph) was a young Bohemian cellist when he journeyed to Dresden (probably about 1925) to audition for the Dresden Symphony, conducted by Richard Strauss. He was successful in the first stages of the audition and was named as a finalist to be auditioned the next day. He apologized to the auditioning committee, explaining that he didn't have money to stay the night. They assured him that they would arrange his housing and food, allowing him to advance to the finals, which he won. He became principal cellist in the Dresden musical establishment and remained there until Hitler's rise to power in Germany.

Mrs. Kratina was the daughter of the American consul to Germany, whose family lived in the Atlanta area. (The consul was in Germany before World War II, living in Dresden.) Somehow, she met Mr. Kratina and eventually became his wife. She was very active socially in Dresden, especially in connection with musical events. She was quite capable of functioning in the complex and highly ordered community of which the consulate was a part. After moving to America she continued to associate with the international community in Atlanta, encouraging the development of all aspects of culture with emphasis upon music. While I was in Atlanta, Mrs. Kratina studied the Hungarian language with a refugee from Hungary who came to her home weekly to teach her. She remarked to me that Hungarian was the most difficult language she had ever studied.

Mrs. Kratina was especially active in the German community of Atlanta. That community had a sort of club for young people who met informally to socialize and to keep their culture active. I was invited to join them, even though I could speak hardly any German. I remember one evening when the meeting was really a dance.

Music for dancing was provided by an LP recording featuring an ensemble called the *Munich Mountaineers*. They had recorded their impression of American country music! As I listened and tried to dance, I could hardly stop laughing: I couldn't understand how they could so completely misunderstand musical style. I was concerned that I might be insulting my friends in the club, but I was helpless to control the laugh impulse.

At one of the club meetings, I met the lovely *Ildico Spaeneth*, visiting niece of the German consul. I invited her on dates several times during her visit in the United States. One of the dates was particularly memorable.

My Ford had developed the nasty habit of wearing out starter motors. To avoid being stranded, I parked the car on a slope so that I could simply push it off, let it coast to build sufficient speed, and pop the clutch to turn the engine and start it. I prepared for the problem when I took Ms. Spaeneth to her uncle's home at the end of the date. (The new Druid Hills Subdivision had several convenient slopes.)

We sat in the car and visited for a while before I escorted her to the front door. We said good night and I returned to the car, only to find that the starter wouldn't work! Not to worry! I would simply push the car off and start it. There was one important detail that I hadn't considered: it was winter, and the mud around my tires had frozen so that I couldn't push off!

I was forced to ring the consul's doorbell at about 11:00 p.m. He came to the door, dressed in his nightgown and wearing a tasseled sleeping cap. (Ildico had already retired.) I explained my problem to him, and he seemed not at all nonplussed, as though such things happened every night. He came out to the car, helped me push it, waved, and returned to his warm home! I decided it was time to trade cars.

A few days later, I happened to drive past Wagstaff Motors, an automobile dealer in Atlanta. On a whim, I decided to stop and see what might be available to me. They were just finishing the paperwork on a two-tone blue 1953 Plymouth two-door hardtop that they were receiving as a trade-in. I asked about trading my Ford for it, and they offered to trade for 875 dollars balance if I would accept the Plymouth before it went through their reconditioning shop. I looked the car over carefully and saw that it was in nearly-new condition, cleaner than I usually kept my car. I accepted the deal, filled out the paperwork, and drove to the Kratina home in my "new" car. *Their* car was a 1954 Plymouth, almost like mine with a few small differences in style. Both had fluid drives, sort of like half of an automatic transmission. It was not necessary to use the clutch when stopping, and the car would start from a halt in any gear (somewhat slowly). We congratulated each other on our exceptional taste and judgment in selecting a car.

Friedrich Kratina was the only son of the Kratinas. A medical doctor, he lived away from Atlanta and never visited while I was there. He was often mentioned affectionately, and I heard the story of his early life. He was born in Dresden a few years before Hitler's surge to power. At an early age, it became likely that he would be enlisted in the Youth Corps, something that his parents wished to avoid. They managed to smuggle him out of the country on a pretext, and when they knew he was safely outside of Germany they also left, never to return. (They managed to ship a houseful of furniture, including much of the famous Dresden china, to Atlanta, where they furnished the Ansley Park house with it.)

The fourth member of the Kratina household was Elsa, the cook and housekeeper. Born in Saxony, she became a servant to the Kratinas in 1932, the year of my birth. Her relationship to the Kratinas was complex and difficult for me to understand. She was loved and treated as a member of the family, yet she was expected to behave in the manner I associated with the servant class. When we were walking on the street, Elsa walked ten paces behind the Kratinas, and she always addressed Mr. Kratina as "Herr Kratina." Mrs. Kratina was *gnadige frau* ("dear and gracious lady"). Elsa could be described very well as "cute." She was rather short and pleasingly plump, although by no means fat. She tended to speak in the dialect of Saxony, which I gathered was rustic German comparable to Tennessee English of the 1930s. Mr. Kratina often spoke to Elsa in her dialect, which I could barely distinguish, and Elsa would break into uncontrollable laughter. (I was immediately subjected to a rule: when I ate with the Kratinas, I must speak in German to ask for anything I wanted. In this way, I learned quite a lot of practical, everyday German. I vowed to learn more, but I never did!)

Elsa was a masterful cook. She prepared all meals in the Kratina household, but she gave virtuoso performances for the frequent dinner parties. I am sure that most of her dishes were standard fare at banquets in prewar Austria, but they were completely new to me. I remember especially a spinach dish that had the consistency of mashed potatoes and was embellished with grated boiled egg, a dish consisting of a whole fish (pike or sturgeon) that looked as if it were swimming in milk in a large shallow serving dish, fantastic desserts of many kinds, and many other dishes that I can't remember but thoroughly appreciated at the time. Mr. Kratina's favorite was Pflaumen-Knodle, a Bavarian dish meant to accompany roast duck or other meat dishes. It was made of a potato dough rolled out like pie crust, cut into strips that were wrapped around plum halves, cooked in water until the plums were tender, and then fried in butter and sprinkled with powdered sugar. I remember one family dinner when nothing else was served except coffee or milk. Mr. Kratina ate with great relish!

The Kratina house was furnished in antique wood furniture from Dresden, rather dark and heavy in appearance. Mr. Kratina's studio held an ancient wood music stand built for a string quartet. Four candleholders arranged alternately with music desks were meant to provide light for the performers, although Mr. Kratina actually *used* electric lights. Four chairs and a piano completed the furnishings in the room. The walls were covered with snapshots and correspondence from his early days in Germany. Richard Strauss appeared with Mr. Kratina in many of the photos, and handwritten notes from him were plentiful on the walls. There were also such notes from members of the aristocracy thanking Mr. Kratina for performing at their invitation in various recitals and other events. It was conventional in those days for members of the aristocracy to "invite" artists to perform at their castles. Artists understood that refusal without very good reason was inexcusable. There was no pay as such for performances. Instead, the performers would receive medals (usually gold). It was perfectly acceptable for the artists to sell the medals for their considerable worth in melted gold. Mr. Kratina had several such medals attached to the walls of his studio.

Although retired, Mr. Kratina practiced the cello every day. I would wake to the sound of his practicing on the magnificent Nicolo Gagliano, which he had owned for many years. I would lazily drag myself out of bed (I slept upstairs), get dressed, and go down for breakfast, knowing that I would hear the admonishment *"Die morgen stunde hat gold im mund"* ("The morning hours have gold in their mouths"). I also practiced every day, but I began later!

Mr. Kratina kept up his musical life in the community, doing some teaching at home and serving as a part-time faculty member at the University of Georgia in Athens (which he pronounced "*aah*-tens"). As I remember, he and Hugh Hodgson were the only music faculty members at that school. They taught a course in Music Appreciation each Thursday evening in which they performed music for cello and piano. The repertoire consisted of music from Baroque,

Classical, Romantic, and Contemporary periods. The class must have been taught as a series of lecture-recitals. Mr. Kratina was enthusiastic about the class, often mentioning it in the course of daily activities.

Mr. Kratina also managed to have me invited to perform with him in church and community events in Atlanta. There were many such events since most churches had very active music programs that performed cantatas, oratorios, and seasonal music with choir, organ, and instrumental ensembles. Sometimes, we were invited to play purely instrumental music during the services. Later I realized what an honor it was to be invited to share performances with him! His stunning career had included premier performances of many of the great Richard Strauss works (with Strauss conducting) composed before the war.

Richard Strauss was often maligned, partly because of his association with the Nazi party. His music was said (usually by young graduate assistants teaching Symphonic Literature) to be overblown, overripe Romanticism that was purposely too difficult to play. It was meant to be *al fresco* music—that is, music to be faked (giving the general impression of the notes). Many symphony conductors felt obliged to represent Strauss in one program per year, and they often chose *Til Eulenspiegel's Merry Pranks* for the purpose. Perhaps the choice was related to the relative shortness of the composition or its relative ease of execution: perhaps its relative familiarity and popularity could induce an audience to endure its performance.

I was forced to consider the political implications of Richard Strauss's membership in the Nazi party. Was it necessary to ban his *music* because of his *politics*? Did his music inspire Nazis to torture and murder more Jews or to do so more enthusiastically? Did the cost of his musical activities (paid by the government) reduce the amount of money available to pay for military atrocities? Could it be possible that Nazis who heard his music might have second thoughts about their daily activities and try to find a way out of the many dilemmas they must have experienced? Was Strauss aware that he was born with rare musical gifts and that he had an obligation to create eternal beauty regardless of his earthly surroundings? I was unable to find satisfactory answers to those questions, but I continued to find more and more satisfaction in playing and hearing the *music* of Strauss. I also continued to marvel that circumstances had placed me in the home of one of the musicians who worked with Strauss daily for years, who conversed with him on many subjects as they walked together, and who collaborated importantly in the creation of some of the world's great music.

Such was the condition in the United States until such conductors as Leonard Bernstein and others rehearsed and performed Richard Strauss's music *as it was written.* Suddenly, it was popular! Now excerpts are on the *repertoire* list of practically every symphonic audition and woes betide the performer who tries to fake them!

There were two extra rooms in the Kratina house. I occupied one and Eban Gilbert the other. Mr. Gilbert was a linguist who had recently translated *Gone with the Wind* into Spanish. He was a very distinguished gentleman with polished manners and pleasant disposition. He was married, but he and his wife had an arrangement that was novel to me: she lived and worked in a distant city, and she would visit him in Atlanta as often as possible. After I became acquainted with Mr. Gilbert, we would spend hours talking about many topics, one of which was *dignity.* He made a comment that I haven't forgotten: "I think a person should have dignity, even when sitting on the toilet."

Another time we were talking about the difficulty of translating local idioms into Spanish so that they would make sense. He asked me to give an example for him to translate. I chose "ball-rack sheet rider." He had no idea what that was, so I explained that it was a sort of rack with steel ball bearings. The rack was attached to a multilith printer so that paper would go under the bearings on its way to the printing cylinder. The bearings would smooth the paper to avoid wrinkles and to keep it from jamming. I explained that I had run a multilith for several years to help pay my way through college.

Mr. Gilbert could not find a satisfactory way to translate my phrase into Spanish, but he was immediately interested in my experience running the multilith! His office had such a machine that they hoped to use in duplicating his translations. No one had been able to run it. Could I find eight or ten hours per week to run their machine? I could, and did. I enjoyed the work, and the extra income was welcome.

The Kratinas were devout Roman Catholics, a dangerous persuasion at that time in Atlanta. Rumors circulated that there were gangs of thugs roaming the streets ready to beat up any Catholics they could identify. The Kratinas were cautious going into and out of the church, trying not to be observed. They were especially concerned with Ash Wednesday: they did not want to remove the ashes from their foreheads, even though the ashes would clearly indicate their religious affiliation. Apparently, they didn't consider changing their religious practices in any way except to make them unobtrusive.

Atlanta Symphony rehearsals began soon after I arrived in Atlanta. Our rehearsal room was actually located in a former parking garage, the first building in the new Georgia State University. There were no walls, only heavy curtains enclosing the rehearsal area. There was enough acoustic material to make the room acceptable for the purpose, but the surroundings made our beginning rather inauspicious.

I was placed in the third stand of first violins, which was satisfactory to me. I was new and probably the youngest and least experienced member of the orchestra. Our excellent concertmaster (Robert Harrison) and his assistant (Martin Sauser) were in the front stand, and our manager with his partner were in the second.

We began with the Shostakovich *Fifth Symphony*, First Movement. Although I had not played that symphony in college, we had played many that were as difficult or more so. All of us had been notified of the *repertoire* for the season, and I had practiced my part carefully as usual.

About five minutes into the movement, the first violins have a very disjunct melody, made so by expanding the intervals with inserted octaves. It is quite exposed, especially near the end where it goes to a very high B-flat. I felt confident that I played it correctly, as I am sure several others did, but the first violins as a section played every possible pitch from approximately A-flat to C-sharp, creating truly embarrassing cacophony! Mr. Sopkin yelled "Sons of bitches!"

as he glared menacingly at us. I didn't think he necessarily meant *me*, but I certainly felt included in the insult! And the glare!

Mr. Sopkin possibly didn't know that in Indiana that epithet was reserved as a supreme insult somewhat like throwing down the gauntlet in the middle ages. Any male who was insulted in that manner would reply by striking the speaker with any weapon available, and the ensuing fight might result in severe injury or death. Failure to reply in that manner would result in shunning by every male who knew the person insulted. I didn't know what to do! Trying to run Mr. Sopkin through with my bow somehow seemed excessive, and I had to consider that the *whole first violin section* was insulted! None of them seemed to be preparing to fight. Besides, to be fair, I assumed that Mr. Sopkin *conducted* the right note! I decided that I would simply leave the orchestra, even though I had eagerly anticipated playing for the season before beginning service in the Air Force.

That night at dinner, I announced to the Kratinas that I would be leaving. They seemed shocked and asked why. I told them the story, including literal repetition of the insult (at the dining room table!). They asked me to go to at least one more rehearsal before leaving, which I agreed to do.

At the next rehearsal, Mr. Sopkin apologized for his behavior, and I happily decided to remain in the symphony. I always wondered whether the Kratinas had anything to do with the apology.

The concert season was successful, with at least one rehearsal each day and at least one concert per week. I studied violin with Robert Harrison, our concertmaster, who was helpful to me especially as I learned to relax while playing. He graciously recommended me for several playing engagements, including a Christmas program at Mulberry Methodist Church in Macon where I played the slow movement of *Bruch Concerto* and other music. I also performed as concertmaster in the Georgia State University production of *Amahl and the Night Visitors*. The Atlanta Symphony recorded its first professional recording for Emerson Records, an LP that included the Tchaikovsky *Fourth Symphony*. I had played the same symphony as concertmaster at Indiana University, so I knew it well. I especially appreciated Mr. Sopkin's consideration in conducting the last movement with an appropriate tempo and steady beat, allowing the strings to play the notes without resorting to faking.

Among our distinguished guest soloists was Isaac Stern, who played the Brahms *Violin Concerto*. It was magnificent, as we expected. At the next rehearsal, Mr. Sopkin was still exhilarated about Mr. Stern's playing, and he compared Isaac Stern to us. He suggested that we might as well throw our violins into the Chattahoochee River! I agreed with him in a sense, but then I asked myself who would play the orchestral parts of the Brahms. Was Mr. Stern available for that? (Mr. Sopkin tended somewhat toward exhilaration.)

I was invited to go with Mrs. Kratina to visit a wealthy lady and seek her support in founding an opera company in Atlanta. The lady was most pleasant and gracious. During the conversation, she informed us that she was going to Vienna, Austria, soon for the reopening of the Vienna Opera. The opera house had been heavily damaged during the war, but it was completely restored. She wanted Mrs. Kratina to advise which of two diamond tiaras she should wear. She modeled both for us, and Mrs. Kratina helped her make the choice.

Evidently, our fundraising efforts were successful. The new opera company performed three operas that year in the Woman's Club Auditorium near the Kratina's home. The first production included two short operas: *Cavalleria Rusticana* by Mascagni and *Pagliacci* by Leoncavallo. For the first production, the orchestra consisted of a string quartet, piano, and electronic organ. The second production, *Faust* by Gounod, used a double string quartet (with string bass), flute, oboe, clarinet, bassoon, trumpet, trombone, piano, and organ. Second wind parts were played on organ or cued into parts that were not busy at the moment (tasteful trumpet playing can substitute for second flute, etc.). The ensemble was rather convincing as an orchestra, and the performance was again successful. I played first violin/concertmaster in both productions, and I enjoyed it enormously. (I had played a total of twenty-six operas at Indiana University, often as concertmaster, but we used as many musicians as we could fit into the pit. For *Parsifal*, the orchestra could number eighty to one hundred performers, with three alternate wind sections for replacements during performances. Our pit was on an elevator).

I continued to rehearse and perform with the symphony and to play and teach as opportunities were presented. Uncertain whether there would be more years as a musician, I tried to cram as much joy as possible into my year in Atlanta. I also prepared the Tchaikovsky *Violin Concerto* for audition in case the Air Force delayed my service further, allowing me another season in Atlanta. (That didn't happen.) At the end of the last concert of the season, I said goodbye to my friends and headed my already-loaded car toward Lackland Air Force Base in San Antonio, Texas. Since I had only minimum time for the trip, I didn't bother to change out of my white tie and tails. I would change the next morning at my tourist cabin. I drove about three hours before looking for a place to sleep.

14

The long drive to San Antonio was uneventful. Air-conditioned cars were almost unknown in 1956, certainly to owners of Plymouths! I chose to drive southwest to Mobile, Alabama, then west to San Antonio. The temperature grew hotter and hotter as well as more humid. I stopped for the first night after two or three hours driving, still wearing my formal shirt and trousers. I was relieved to remove them, take a shower, and go to sleep. I wore jeans and a T-shirt for the rest of the trip.

Officers' pre-flight training at Lackland Air Force Base was meant to be a thirty-day program for newly-commissioned officers who were to be assigned to pilot training. We were to become acclimated to military duty, to the customs of the service, and to the relationship of officers to enlisted men (there were no women in the program at that time). Since officers wore custom-made uniforms, we were given a uniform allowance along with instructions concerning number and type of articles of clothing we would need. There was a large uniform manufacturing company near the base. We ordered uniforms immediately to allow time for their manufacture before training ended. Some of our newly-minted second lieutenants bought parts of uniforms from the post exchange and assembled their own, hoping to impress our commander when they reported for duty. They used their own taste in choosing parts, which resulted in some interesting combinations. I know of one young man who mixed summer with winter parts and topped the result with a field-grade hat (lightning bolts on the bill). Our commander, a man of great experience, complimented the young officer's taste, allowing him to discover his blunders and remedy them without losing face.

Our instructor for preflight was a very seasoned black master sergeant (political correctness had not yet been invented: we had never heard the term "African-American"). He introduced himself and gave a memorable short speech: "You gentlemen have been given an honor that I would do anything to receive. You are to serve as officers in the United States Air Force. All of you outrank me, even though I am your instructor. I will respect you as officers. If you order me to pick up a corner of this building [our barracks] I may not pick it up, but I will surely back up to it and grunt!"

We were assigned some routine duties to help us assume our positions as officers. One of these duties was to receive a new group of enlisted men who had arrived the night before. They had received the traditional "buzz" haircut (watching sadly as their treasured "duck-butt" locks tumbled to the floor), had been issued uniforms, and were instructed to empty their pockets on their beds and stand at attention while we searched for forbidden items to confiscate. We circulated among the new enlistees, collecting alcoholic beverages, drugs, weapons ("zip" guns, knives, and brass knuckles), pornographic literature, and any other items not allowed. We filled large garbage bags with such items. Then we read certain paragraphs from the Universal Code of Military Justice, mostly describing homosexual acts. Each paragraph ended with the penalty if found guilty of such acts: death by firing squad. Certainly we had their attention! They looked at us with awe (we were not much older than they), and one of them asked one of us how long we had been on active duty. He answered "two days," which caused the looks of awe to increase!

Our days began early! The bugle sounded and we leapt out of our bunk beds and into the large bathroom (no privacy). We performed the morning "three S" functions that ended with *shave* and *shower* (leaving the third "S" to the imagination). We usually had only five or ten minutes to get to breakfast, which consisted of mostly greasy food (scrambled eggs, bacon or sausage, toast, cereal, coffee, juice). We ate large amounts and very quickly. Then we immediately went to physical conditioning: calisthenics for forty-five minutes followed by a mile run up to a fence and back (in the desert). As I remember it, we were allowed seven minutes for the run. We were dressed in fatigue pants, T-shirts, and flying boots. The boots were necessary protection of our feet from cactus, briars, and an assortment of unfriendly critters (including rattlesnakes). The sand was always hot, and we could feel the heat through our boots. After the morning run, we had a break for an hour or two before our first organized event of the day. Many of us vomited first, took another shower, and went to the PX where we could get food again.

The days were filled with classes and various examinations to establish our physical fitness for military flying. Air force standards were rather severe and were strictly followed. I passed everything except weight: for my height, I must weigh a minimum of 140 pounds. I weighed 139. I was given several days to gain one pound before our final physical examination. This was no easy task since our daily exertions were strenuous and mostly in full sun! I was advised to "eat everything in sight" in the mess hall, to eat between meals, to concentrate upon beef and potatoes, and to eat bananas and drink beer. Also, at the physical exam I should drink all the water I could hold just before weighing. I did all these things, and at the exam, I weighed 141 pounds. I was in!

Several lectures were devoted to military customs and discipline. Some of the customs seemed strange to me: officers in uniform never pushed a baby buggy, carried a baby in their arms, or carried an umbrella. When two or more military men walked on the street, they must move as a military unit in formation and at marching cadence. When two military men met, the lower rank saluted first and the higher rank returned the salute. Officers did not fraternize with enlisted personnel on duty or off. Officers did not lie. Officers were an elite group in the United States just as in foreign countries. Proper military courtesy was a symbol of self-respect and of respect for the chain of command. Good discipline was a requisite of good morale and unit effectiveness.

The welfare of subordinates was of first concern to officers. An officer would not accept comfort and safety for himself until they had been arranged for every subordinate. In combat, the emphasis was upon protecting others rather than self.

The Air Force did not respect heroism as depicted in Hollywood movies. Pilots were expected to be capable of military mission fulfillment as ordered without unnecessary risk to life or property. We were to become professional pilots (with commercial licenses), but our first priority was to be Air Force officers.

Our Air Force assignment was not "just another job," although recruitment efforts often portrayed our military life as comparable to work in industry or business. The United States maintains a military establishment because it is sometimes necessary to destroy property and kill people in defense of national interests. After training, we might be assigned to duty that seemed only remotely related to destroying and killing, but we would be cogs in a giant machine assembled for that purpose. In modern warfare, the line between civilians and military personnel becomes blurred. For example, in World War II, many civilians were killed and their homes demolished both in Germany and England. Military personnel may have been safer than civilians in that conflict.

I felt that the Air Force indoctrinated us well, preparing us for military duty. I noticed almost continual efforts to recruit us as career rather than temporary officers, and I seriously considered changing status and asking for a regular commission. Although I respected the Air Force and wanted to serve honorably, I couldn't give up the career I had already chosen.

The thirty-day preflight was long enough. I didn't particularly like San Antonio (or Texas, for that matter). I was anxious to begin pilot training! I was truly disappointed a few days before our scheduled completion of preflight: I received notice that my chest X-rays had been lost and that I would be assigned to another class to do them again. I would remain at Lackland another thirty days on casual duty! (Somehow I thought they could have simply given me another chest X-ray, but already I knew that the "Air Force way" was the one I would follow.)

Casual duty consisted of breakfast, roll call, calisthenics, the mile run, and being available for any duty that might be assigned.

No duties were assigned, and I was allowed to visit San Antonio as often as I wished. Until that time, I had barely seen San Antonio: it was actually a fine city, and I enjoyed my frequent trips there.

One of my favorite places in San Antonio was the River Walk. At that time, it was practically undeveloped, except for the walk itself. There were many shops and Mexican restaurants along the way. Everyone was friendly! I had not seen many Mexicans before, but I had read rather uncomplimentary descriptions in western novels. Mexicans were usually depicted as undesirables, enemies of the cowboy hero. The only Mexican women in such novels were usually young, impossibly attractive, and available to the hero. They usually fell in love, but the cowboy rode off into the sunset rather than getting married. This image was, of course, completely inaccurate (except the impossibly attractive part).

I found a family-owned Mexican restaurant somewhere along the River Walk. Both parents worked there, and there were several sons and one daughter. All of them played instruments and sang so that they often performed on a small platform while the customers ate. I discovered Mexican food at that restaurant, and I liked it! (Previously, I had tasted and enjoyed Joe's hot tamales on the streets of Bloomington, Indiana, where Joe sold them.) I visited that restaurant several times each week.

The family and I became acquainted. All were friendly, but the young daughter seemed more so. I judged her to be about fourteen years old, much too young for the fantasies that began to trouble me. I could have been tempted to abandon my determination to remain single until after my Air Force duties, but somehow, I managed to keep our relationship on the *just friendly* level. Perhaps it was fortunate that my thirty days of casual duty came to an end.

I was ordered to Marianna Air Force Base in Florida for primary pilot training. The base was a civilian contract school that had been formed for the purpose. All instruction was by civilians with administration by military officers. I would be a member of Class 57-P. I loaded my newly-acquired uniforms, my much-neglected violin, and my other personal belongings into the Plymouth and headed for Marianna, Florida.

15

In 1956, Marianna, Florida, was a very small town twenty-six air miles south of Dothan, Alabama. It was also about fifty miles west of Tallahassee, Florida, the location of Florida State University and a nurses' school that was well known to student pilots. The Marianna community consisted mostly of peanut farms, and the local citizenry was made up of farm families and a few business and professional families as expected in such a community. The air base was a few miles from Marianna. Its runways are still there, serving as a community airport. Our base housing is also still there, mixed now with other buildings. My wife and I visited a few years ago, and I was able to recognize my living quarters, the air field, the control tower, and many other features that were present when I was in primary training. The tower operator at the airport told me that many former student pilots visit there often to renew old memories, much like the former adjutant who visits his World War II base in England at the beginning of the movie *Twelve O'clock High*.

Approaching Marianna, it was necessary to cross the Chipola River, but there was no bridge! Crossing was by ferry boat, which was powered by a twenty-five-horsepower outboard motor. I looked at the motor with considerable mistrust, but the operator seemed quite sure that we could make the voyage of about two hundred feet. Upon closer examination, I found that the boat was attached to a heavy cable that stretched between the two docks, and the water current was so slow as to be almost imperceptible. I had little choice but to trust the arrangement, so with misgivings I drove my Plymouth onto the boat, and we cast off. A few minutes later, we arrived at the other side with no mishaps. Another new experience!

I arrived at the air base at dusk. I could see the buildings from a distance, and the arrangement looked new and attractive. I checked in and went to the Officer's Club for a fine dinner. The sound system was playing themes from recent movies, including *Picnic*.

Our BOQ (bachelor officer quarters) buildings were arranged in suites each of which contained two bedrooms separated by a generously-sized bath. Each bedroom was shared by two officers. My roommate was Lt. Richard L. Kocher from Los Angeles, California. He was an English major in college who hoped to become a professor of English after his service in the Air Force. He was quite familiar with music, and our tastes were similar. A devout Catholic, he enjoyed hearing about my religious experiences, although he found my ignorance of Catholicism alarming and perplexing. After we became acquainted, he told me, "When we get to the pearly gates, St. Peter is going to let you in because you're so damned ignorant, but he's going to send me to purgatory for a few years because I failed to convert you." We both received the same assignments through basic pilot training and duty in Strategic Air Command. After we were released, we tried unsuccessfully to remain in contact. I consider him one of my best friends.

Flight training began the day after I arrived. There were student officers and student cadets (high school graduates who were allowed to complete flight training before receiving their commissions). Each instructor was assigned four student pilots. We flew in the morning and attended ground school in the afternoon for a week and then switched in order to allow us to experience as many different conditions as possible.

My first instructor was Robert Wildman, a soft-spoken man who flew our planes the way I would like to be able to play the violin. He had begun his flying career as a crop-duster, flying Stearman biplanes loaded with insecticide for many hours per day during the short seasons. He confided to me that sometimes he was so tired he didn't bother to pull up sufficiently to completely clear the trees at the ends of rows: he simply allowed his landing gear to drag through the top branches! He could teach as well as he could fly. With his help, we gained proficiency quickly and built our confidence at the same time. Each of his four students flew approximately one hour per day: debriefing was done by all four at the ends of the flying periods. We learned from each other.

After a brief introduction, Mr. Wildman took us to the flight line to meet our first trainer plane, the Beech T-34. We soon realized that the Air Force had provided us with "the Cadillac of trainers"! It was a military (two-place) version of the civilian Beech *Debonair* (four-place). (I am certain that there were more differences between the two planes than we could perceive.)

Mr. Wildman demonstrated how to preflight the T-34, emphasizing flight safety. We always used checklists, even after we had memorized them. It was easy to make potentially fatal mistakes regardless of the amount of our flying experience. After the preflight, it was time to fly!

When it was my turn to fly, I climbed into the front seat (by that time very familiar because we were required to spend many hours in the cockpit memorizing instruments and controls so that blindfolded we could touch them instantly). After checking that I was correctly buckled in and the seatbelt sufficiently tightened, Mr. Wildman started the engine. He taxied out to the active runway, received clearance for takeoff from the tower, advanced the throttle, and began the takeoff roll, describing all his actions and the reasons for them during the process. After a short roll, he rotated (pulled back) the control stick to raise the nose into takeoff position and allowed the plane to fly itself off the runway at about fifty-five knots airspeed. We were flying! I remembered watching the Aeronca Champions at Monroe County Airport years before, but this time, I was inside looking out!

We flew one traffic pattern, landed, and taxied back to the end of the active runway. "Now *you're* going to do it," Mr. Wildman said. *Now?* Somehow I had thought I might fly in a few days or perhaps a week, but *now?* "I'll talk you through it." Mr. Wildman said it with such confidence that I knew I could do it.

Mr. Wildman calmly told me every move to make, taxiing into takeoff position, getting clearance from the tower, pressing right rudder to counter engine torque, advancing the throttle smoothly to avoid unnecessary engine abuse, steering the plane as it gained speed, rotating at fifty-five knots, and allowing the plane to fly off the runway. I can't express or even describe the feelings of satisfaction I experienced as the wheels left the runway and I retracted the landing gear! One of my ambitions had been reached that day! Somehow a degree of that same feeling returned every time I took off after that. I suspect that all pilots have similar experiences.

Mr. Wildman talked me through flap retraction, power reduction, traffic pattern flying, and prelanding checklist. (I still have a copy of the T-34 checklist. It looks clean and new: I had worn out several.) When we were lined up for landing, he supervised power setting and the change to "three-point" attitude as we approached landing. "Now do a straight-ahead power-off stall," he said. I did it, and we were on the runway. A grease job! (So smooth we couldn't feel the touchdown, but we could hear the tires squeak.) We made the landing a "touch-and-go" and did several more takeoffs and landings, the last one a "full stop." We taxied back to our parking space and performed the engine shutdown checklist. My first flying lesson was finished! Successfully!

We flew every day if weather permitted. Sometimes we would arrive at the flight line when it was overcast, but we expected it to "burn off" in an hour or two. We were introduced to basic maneuvers such as change of airspeed, slow flight, clearing turns, climb and level-off, power letdown (being careful not to abuse the engine by sudden heating/cooling), stalls and recovery, and many traffic patterns and landings. After I had received a total of about eight hours of flight instruction, we landed, cleared the runway, and stopped on the taxi strip. Mr. Wildman said, "Take the plane and make three landings. I'll watch from the tower and help you if necessary." I was soloing! There was no fanfare and "solo" was not mentioned, but I felt as if the whole world was watching. I did as Mr. Wildman instructed: two touch-and-goes and one full-stop landing. Later, Mr. Wildman noted in his critique "first landing just short of the runway." I was cleared for solo flight!

The T-34 was a very stable aircraft. It would fly all standard aer-obatics, but somewhat reluctantly. It wanted to fly straight and level, to make coordinated turns, and to take off and land without inci-dent. It didn't want to spin, but it would. We were taught two-turn precision spins and recoveries, but actually, the plane would recover by itself if we simply released the controls. We used section lines on the ground as references so that we knew exactly where we were in all maneuvers. (Before pilot training, I didn't know there *were* section lines.) We learned chandelles, lazy-eights, loops, aileron rolls, barrel rolls, Cuban eights, Immelmann turns, and vertical recoveries. After takeoff and traffic clearance, we were seldom right-side up until time to land. We were not allowed to do snap-rolls, and we were to avoid negative Gs. We were constantly reminded that we could not know too much about weather, aircraft systems, or aerodynamics. We were to learn the limitations of our aircraft and ourselves: we were never to exceed or even approach those limitations except in rare emergencies.

Many days were clear, with towering cumulous clouds scattered from one horizon to the other. We often flew aerobatics between clouds, being careful to allow enough clearance to avoid collisions. I enjoyed flying loops that began on one side of a cloud and more or less circled it vertically. I often reflected upon how much progress I had made in a very short time, wondering how much further I could go and how long it would take. There were no guarantees that we could finish pilot training and receive our wings: quite a few of our number were "washed out" (dropped from the program because of perceived weaknesses as potential pilots). I remember one friend who experienced that fate: he had soloed in the T-34 before his instructors discovered that he suffered from vertigo. He could not distinguish "up" from "down" visually, a rather dangerous condition for a pilot! He was treated with respect by everyone: he had given flying training all he had to give. Any of us could have suffered a similar fate.

Forced landings were not exactly maneuvers, but we learned them well! At any point in any flight, the instructor could retard the throttle and announce "forced landing." We did this at least once in every flight—sometimes twice or more. The procedure was to establish correct glide speed, try to re-tart the engine if time permitted, select a satisfactory place to land, and set up an approach which would bring us to the place without power. Instructors would initiate forced-landing practice at the most awkward moments in our flight. We would glide as though we were actually going to land, but the instructor brought in the power at his discretion, never allowing the plane to touch ground (quite). We would often overtake peanut farmers, fly just in front of their tractors, apply power, and climb heavenward with a mighty roar! The farmers were unaware of our presence until they heard the sound and saw us materialize directly in front of them. Their heads would snap upwards as they saw us, providing some entertainment for the more sadistic pilots (probably also causing some sore necks for peanut farmers).

We finished the curriculum in T-34s and graduated to the T-28. Although we still respected the T-34, we began speaking of it as the "Mickey Mouse" airplane; the T-28 was similar in appearance and performance to a World War II fighter.

There were two versions of the T-28: the Air Force and the US Navy versions (in use for Navy flight training at Pensacola, Florida). Because the Navy planned to use the plane for carrier training, it was necessary to "beef up" the airframe and add a tail-hook. This added weight to the plane, requiring a larger engine. The Air Force version had a single-row radial engine originally designed by the company that made Kaiser-Frazier automobiles. (They designed the engine for a light tank, which was not accepted by the military.) That engine had the nasty habit of simply stopping at any point in a flight. Usually, it would start running again after a disconcerting few seconds. (My instructor and I experienced this once on a day cross-country flight. We were over Opelika, Alabama, where nothing was visible below except pine trees. We were tightening our parachute harnesses, preparing to bail out, when the engine calmly began producing power again as though nothing untoward had happened! We continued to Marianna and landed without further incident.)

The T-28 was much faster that the T-34. Our normal cruise speed was 150 knots (about 172 miles per hour) and the never-exceed speed was 367 knots. The plane was also much less stable than the T-34, which made aerobatics easier to perform, including spins.

(We *had* to use spin recovery procedures to perform the precision two-turn spin and recovery, which we had learned in the T-34.) To allow for its greater speed and use of altitude, we remained above 5,000 feet in the practice area, leaving the lower altitudes for the T-34s. The T-28 was also intended to imitate the handling characteristics of the T-33 (jet) trainer, which was in use for basic single-engine training. Takeoff without flaps in the T-28 was very much like takeoff *with* flaps in the T-33. We continued to practice everything in the T-28 that we had learned in the T-34, adding four items to the curriculum: 360-degree overhead approaches to landing, instrument flying, night flying, and night cross-country flying.

I doubted that I could do any of the four new items in the curriculum, but I had managed to learn quite a lot about flying since my arrival at Marianna. I kept telling myself, *One step at a time!*

The T-28 landed like a fighter plane. Initial approach was at traffic pattern altitude straight-in toward the landing runway. Over the runway numbers, the plane was banked sixty degrees (usually to the right), and the throttle was closed until the landing-gear warning horn sounded. A 180-degree turn was executed, the wings were leveled, and the landing gear extended. Altitude and airspeed were allowed to dissipate. Opposite the desired landing spot three-quarter flaps were lowered, and a right turn was initiated, "playing" the turn to roll out at the desired final approach altitude and direction. The throttle was used to control altitude as the airspeed gradually diminished for landing. Although this was not easy, I found that I could learn it, and I did.

Instrument training was done with the student in the back seat, allowing the instructor to maintain clearance from other planes and obstacles. A collapsible canvas hood enclosed the student pilot so that only instruments and controls were visible from the beginning of the takeoff roll. The entire period of instruction was completed under the hood with simulated clearances from the instructor until the plane was on short final approach. At that point, the student was allowed to remove the hood and complete the landing. Forced landings were not practiced on such flights, but recoveries from unusual attitudes were done. The student pilot was instructed to close his eyes while the instructor flew the plane in an uncoordinated manner until it was in an unusual attitude (often upside down). At that point, the instructor would say, "You have it," and the student would open his eyes and begin recovery. I heard stories about students who "recovered" perfectly in every way except one: they were inverted!

I *knew* that I could not learn to fly at night! My instructor had other ideas. On the first night that was scheduled for flying, we did the usual preflight inspection, and I climbed into the front cockpit as usual. We did our usual warm-up and engine check. I received clearance and took the active runway. I released the brakes and advanced the throttle to takeoff setting. Although we couldn't see the runway, it was clearly outlined by blue lights. (I hoped there was no debris for us to hit.) When we reached takeoff airspeed, I rotated as usual and could see—*nothing!* There was *no horizon!* Only inky blackness! We had talked about this in ground training, and my shock at seeing it lasted only seconds. It was as though I heard Mr. Wildman say, "Keep your wings level and refer to instruments. When you have a positive rate of climb, retract the landing gear. At three hundred feet altitude, clear the traffic pattern (ninety-degree left and right turns) and climb to upper-traffic pattern altitude. Enter the upper traffic pattern and remain in it, making circuits around the active runway at normal cruise speeds for one hour. After one hour, exit the upper traffic pattern, enter the normal pattern, and make a full-stop landing." As I followed the instructions, I began to glance outside the aircraft. Even though the horizon was not clear, I could easily see the blue runway lights and the red approach lights. I could also see the clearance lights on each plane in the traffic pattern as well as the lights from the buildings on the base, the lights on the highways, and the lights of Marianna. I thought, *Hey, you're flying at night! You thought you couldn't do this! You're even able to think of other things as you fly! Maybe you're not so bad at this, after all!* We landed and my instructor cleared me for solo night flight!

The last thing that I *knew I couldn't do* was night solo cross-country. We were to fly to Montgomery, Alabama, and return. Although I had by that time driven such distances in my Plymouth many times, flying there and back seemed magical to me, even though no strange-field landing was planned. When the time came, I climbed into my assigned plane and took off, not willing to bet that I would ever return!

By that time, I knew that it was very unlikely that I would encounter enough wind in such a short distance to take me far from my planned route. It would not be necessary to work a navigation problem on my E-6B calculator while flying the plane with my knees, as I had done on my day solo cross-country. That little exercise had taken me forty degrees off-course, resulting in my circling Spence Air Force Base in Moultrie, Georgia, until a rather sarcastic instructor intercepted me in a T-28 and led me to Marianna, Florida. I will never forget his comment as I entered the traffic pattern at Marianna. "Do you think you can find your base now?" I will also never forget the feeling of disgrace I felt when I had landed and parked on our flight line. Fortunately, everyone else had left the flight line and gone to dinner. My instructor met me and said, "Vern, I'm surprised at you." At least, he was *surprised!* (I wasn't.) Under the circumstances, there were only three answers available to me: "Yes, sir!" "No, sir!" "Sorry, sir!" I chose the third answer, thinking it the most appropriate.

I took off for Montgomery after vowing to utilize a better combination of theory and practice than I had on my first (day) solo cross-country. Shortly after takeoff, I noticed an orange glow coming from my engine on both sides, in fact seeming to circle the engine! An engine fire? Should I bail out? *"Not just yet,"* I heard a voice say. (It sounded just like Mr. Wildman!) *"Why not repeat your after-takeoff checklist?"* I did, and I had forgotten to close the cowl-flaps! Whadda I do now? *"You might try closing them."* I did. *"Now, check your cylinder-head temperature."* I did. Slightly low. *"Just watch it. It will probably be normal in a few minutes."* It was, and I gained confidence that cowl flaps were on the plane for a purpose other than the harassment of student pilots, and that they worked if operated appropriately. I turned on course to Montgomery.

After such a frantic beginning, I started to relax and look outside the aircraft for other reasons than avoiding a collision. It *was* a beautiful night, with millions of stars, a few high clouds, and apparently no wind. I began to understand why so many pilots have highly developed aesthetic sensibilities: they are constantly surrounded by reality, with its unadulterated risks and rewards. (The practical design of an aircraft suited to its mission results in a work of art.) They (could I presume to say *we?*) continually make decisions that deal with forces much larger than themselves, forces that can most easily be explained by reference to a *higher power*. In a short time, I passed Dothan, Alabama, the limit of our practice area. I thought I could begin to see the lights of Montgomery in the distance. Distances seem to be shortened at night.

I arrived over Montgomery, some eight thousand feet below. I could easily see the outline of the entire city as if I were looking at a moving map. Briefly, I asked myself what I was doing here over a rather large city with an airplane strapped to my rear end. Only a few years earlier, I had impressed my grandmother in Indiana by flying a small model that I assembled with a .039 glow-plug engine and which I could maneuver with a control line! I really haven't had enough time to mature enough to be here! Yet there I was, and it was time to turn back toward Marianna.

The return trip was easier than the flight to Montgomery. I had enough confidence to actually enjoy most of it, often reminding myself to concentrate and not screw it up. (I had seen how easily *that* can be done!) I entered the traffic pattern and landed. My last impossible task had been completed! I had only a month to hone my skills and prepare for my final check ride, this time with a military instructor. (Until that time, I had flown only with civilian instructors, although we practiced strict military discipline.)

One morning, I was on the flight line preparing to fly. I ate a small snack at a little stand placed there for the convenience of pilots who felt hungry and didn't have time to go to the PX. James (Jimmy) Logsdon was there also, and we chatted for a few minutes. He was in the class ahead of mine (57-O), and he had completed all instruction including his final check ride. He was planning to fly the required last flight of about twenty minutes, just one traffic pattern and landing. We both caught the flight-line transportation trailer and rode out to our planes. We said "See you later" and began our preflight inspections.

After I landed, I noticed that our classroom building was full of students and instructors. Several were outside looking at the sky. I asked what was going on and was told that there had been an accident. Two T-28s with solo students had collided, and one was in the traffic pattern preparing to land. Instructors were in radio contact with him. They told him to climb to a safe altitude and they would help to make sure his plane was capable of landing with the damage it had received. They instructed him to lower his landing gear, extend flaps to landing configuration, and reduce power to landing speed. They then took him through several maneuvers so that they could decide whether to attempt a landing or have him bail out. He did several turns and a few stalls, power on and off. The plane seemed controllable, so they instructed him to follow their directions for a straight-in landing. Fire trucks and ambulances were placed strategically, ready to give any possible help. The student made a perfect approach and landing, stopped his plane on the runway, and climbed out. In the collision, his right wing had struck the other plane, removing about three feet of metal skin. I didn't see any other damage. We all returned to the "ready" room. We heard the announcement that one plane had crashed, and we were waiting for all planes to land in order to identify the missing pilot. Finally all but one plane had landed and parked. We were informed that the missing pilot was Jimmy Logsdon and that he had been killed when his plane crashed. Jimmy! I had seen him and talked with him just a short time ago.

That evening, several of us visited the site of the crash. It was in the abundant scrub-brush of North Florida, only a few miles from Marianna. As we approached the site, no plane was visible. When we arrived, we found a ragged hole about ten feet deep and perhaps thirty feet long. The intense heat of the estimated five-hundred knots crash had totally destroyed all but the engine and a few pieces of landing gear. The rest of the site was covered by bits of aluminum, which looked like chewing-gum wrappers. Jimmy's body had been found a short distance from the site. It had struck the ground so hard that it indented the sand about four inches. His parachute had partially opened, but apparently, he had not pulled the rip-cord. Investigators believed that he had attempted to bail out or had been somehow thrown out of the plane at an altitude too low for the chute to fully open. It appeared that his chute had struck the tail of his plane, damaging the chute and causing it to partially open.

All of us had to adjust to our first, but not last, loss of human life as a result of military service. Jimmy was married, which reinforced my resolve not to be married until my Air Force commitment was finished. He was well-liked and respected by everyone who knew him. He believed in the cause for which he died. I tried to imagine how I would want my friends to feel if a similar incident ended my life (is a distinct possibility). Every time we throttled up for takeoff, there was a possibility that we would not be there to throttle back.

I believed that all or nearly all of us were in the military for a similar reason (in addition to Universal Military Training): we believed that for the United States the best assurance of peace was a strong military that would dissuade anyone from attacking us. (This meant that our leaders should be of the highest moral character, sophisticated, intelligent, and compassionate. What a responsibility for voters!) We did not desire war or believe in it: we hoped to "buy time" long enough for the human race to discover a better way to solve problems. We did not want to be wounded or to die, but we knew that the burden of warfare usually fell to young men because they were the only ones capable of bearing it. We also knew that not everyone was capable of flying a combat aircraft, and we believed that those who *were* capable had a responsibility to contribute to the overall mission of the Air Force. We wanted a rather *mundane* life, but we understood that if we placed ourselves "in harm's way" we must accept the resulting conditions. We did not respect "heroics," but we recognized that some of us would be placed in conditions that might cause others to regard us as heroes.

We knew that we would be flying the day after Jimmy's death. It was psychologically the best course of action. Had we taken a day or more off, we might have lost our nerve, and some might never have flown again. I remember flying perhaps more cautiously than usual, seeking to rediscover the wonder and beauty of flying. It was almost as though we were offering a tribute to Jimmy.

I completed my primary training and survived my final check ride. My check pilot criticized everything I did, causing me to think that I had failed, but in the end, I passed. A few days later, I made my final flight and was allowed a short leave before beginning Basic Flight Training. I had been assigned to multiengine training at Reese Air Force Base in Lubbock, Texas, flying TB-25s. It was my choice: I wanted to be qualified to fly for the airlines after military service if I couldn't find a position as a violinist.

16

As I arrived at Reese Air Force Base, my first impression was rather positive. Reese was older than the base at Marianna, Florida. The buildings were strictly military, and there was no hint of landscaping. The first view of the base included a large pond, which invited the newcomer to a swim, but I found out later that swimming would not be enjoyable: the pond was for sewage treatment. All the sewage produced on the base was released into the pond, where decomposition was allowed to take place. Periodically, the resulting sludge was dredged out and allowed to dry in the withering Texas sunlight. After drying, it was used as fertilizer. We were assured that the finished product was completely safe for use and that it didn't smell bad at all! I rather admired that modern method of solving an ancient problem.

At the entrance gate was a parked B-25, permanently on display as a reminder of the dangers of flying into thunderstorms. It was completely covered by dents made when huge hailstones struck it while flying. I could hardly believe such damage could result from hail until I experienced such a thunderstorm (safely on the ground and under a roof). The extremely fortunate crew managed to land at Reese. The B-25 was considered not repairable but very suitable for display.

Unmarried student officers were assigned quarters in ordinary military barracks buildings, which had been adapted for the purpose. The arrangements were much like those at Marianna: two bedrooms, a small kitchen, and a bath comprised a suite. Each bedroom accommodated two officers. The kitchens were hardly used: our refrigerator was empty except for one bottle of vodka whose owner I didn't know.

Lubbock, Texas, was a dry town. Many citizens (including some lovely young ladies) enjoyed being invited to the base Officer's Club for dinner, which could include alcoholic drinks. Air Force personnel could buy beer, wine, and hard liquor at the PX. We also could invite guests to visit our quarters. I invited several young people from the Church of Christ to have lunch with me one Sunday afternoon. They were very interested in the base, the B-25s, and the dinner, but none of us drank alcohol. I discovered that civilians tended to regard Air Force officers, especially pilots, with a degree of awe. This was difficult for me to understand, but I went along with it (even *enjoyed* it). One young lady opened our refrigerator and saw the bottle of vodka. Assuming it was mine, she rather scoldingly said to her boyfriend, "See, some people in our church drink! Why do you have to be so strict?" I didn't bother to explain.

Flight training began almost immediately after our arrival. We learned that our group commander was Colonel Travis Hoover, famous for being the pilot of the second B-25 to take off from the deck of the aircraft carrier *Hornet* behind General "Jimmy" Doolittle on the bombing raid of Tokyo early in World War II. (This raid was featured in the movie *Thirty Seconds over Tokyo*.) Our squadron commander was Major Frederick Shriner, whom we soon met and immediately respected. Captain Yuhas was commander of our flight, the 3501st (Dust Devils). My instructor was 2/Lt. Lionel J. Martoccia, a very capable pilot and instructor who was also a fine trumpet player.

We soon learned why *Dust Devils* was an appropriate name for our flight. The Lubbock area experienced frequent dust storms with dust so thick we could drive our cars only by reference to the edge of the highway. Headlights were useless, except for warning other drivers of our presence. Flying in those conditions was difficult: we could see the runways vertically from traffic pattern altitude, but as we descended to land, visibility was greatly reduced. Aircraft maintenance was also problematic because the engines had to run in extremely dusty conditions.

Soon after I arrived at Reese, the worst thunderstorm I had ever seen passed directly over the base. Fortunately, all personnel were inside buildings as shards of ice larger than my double fists covered the entire area. The B-25s were parked on the ramp as usual. All of them were damaged by hail, the cloth-covered control surfaces shredded as though cut by knives. Flying was suspended for a few days while repairs were made. Cars that were parked outside were covered with dents from the falling ice. My Plymouth was damaged severely, but fortunately, the cost was covered by insurance. My car received new paint, and it looked great!

Lieutenant Martoccia told me that the Air Force discovered he was a trumpeter soon after he joined the service. They immediately assigned him to temporary duty (TDY) trips to play *taps* at military funerals. He played more than 250 such funerals, becoming more and more emotional at each. Finally, he was weeping so much he could hardly play. He asked to be relieved of such assignments: his request was granted.

The TB-25 was the light bomber all of us had seen in World War II combat movies. Our planes had all guns, turrets, and bomb racks removed. We usually flew in groups of three or four (an instructor with two or three students). We could change seats in the air, each student receiving about an hour of instruction. When we weren't at the controls, we carefully observed the instruction of other students, learning as much as possible. Sometimes we were allowed to ask questions if that didn't interfere with instruction.

All that we had learned in Primary Training was utilized in the B-25. We could not do aerobatics, and we didn't practice forced landings, but these were replaced by maneuvers characteristic of twin-engine planes, especially engine-out procedures and single-engine landings.

Twin-engine planes exhibit problems not found in those with a single engine. If one engine loses power for any reason during flight, the pilot must make some quick decisions: identify the problem engine, control the heading with rudder, feather the *correct* propeller, trim the plane for asymmetric thrust, advance the throttle on the good engine to maintain or exceed minimum single-engine airspeed, and deploy the engine fire extinguisher if necessary. All this must be done very quickly, and both pilot and copilot must function well as a team to accomplish it. We practiced these procedures many times at altitude. Sometimes the instructor would set power to simulate single-engine flight, but we also practiced actual feathering procedures. The instructor would initiate the procedures by retarding a throttle and announcing "engine out."

We often practiced simulated single-engine takeoffs and landings. The primary concern in a single-engine takeoff is airspeed. Below minimum single engine airspeed, it is impossible to control the plane and continue flight. It is necessary to reduce power and dive to gain airspeed or to reduce power and make an unplanned landing. Single-engine landings require a commitment to *land* at a certain point when airspeed is too low to go around on one engine.

One afternoon, our flight had just taken off and cleared the traffic pattern when we heard the ominous announcement on the radio: "There has been an actual crash on the field. All aircraft remain clear of the traffic pattern until further notice." We looked down at the base and saw a column of heavy, black smoke. Some smart aleck said on the radio "Scratch one T-Bird," assuming that our recently-arrived T-33 had crashed. We continued the instruction period as scheduled, hearing that the field had been reopened during the period. We made our landing as planned and were informed about the accident.

An instructor and his students were practicing a simulated single-engine landing. Apparently, the student allowed the airspeed to diminish too much and the instructor didn't take control until too late. The plane was undershooting the runway, flying toward the Officers' Club, where a group of wives was meeting. The instructor had no option except to turn the plane and dive into the ground several hundred feet from the club. Everyone aboard was killed, but no one on the ground was injured. This was my second experience witnessing death associated with military flying.

The B-25 was a tricycle gear plane (it had a nosewheel and two main wheels). It was a very sturdy aircraft, but the nosewheel had to be treated with respect. This was especially true in touch-and-go landings. When such a landing was made the aircraft would be "trimmed" for landing and the trim must be changed before allowing the plane to takeoff again. The pilot had to keep the nosewheel off the runway while setting the trim and advancing the throttle for takeoff. This required a considerable amount of strength in the left arm. Instructors were very observant of this particular technique: allowing the nosewheel to bang on the runway might cause the front wheel to collapse with disastrous results. One of the cartoons in our class yearbook showed a student pilot with an enormous left bicep and a normal right one. All of us appreciated the meaning of that cartoon!

Every new officer at Reese had to complete a staff-study as a part of his training. This was required because junior officers were often utilized by commanders to do the "legwork" required in making routine decisions that are necessary to the operation of an air base. There was a required process in the preparation of a staff-study: state the problem, outline the study we had made, and make several recommendations for resolution. I was assigned to study the Drum and Bugle Corps at Reese.

That organization played for public functions at Reese. The most frequent of such functions were Saturday morning parades, which required the participation of everyone assigned to the base. We were always in the starched uniform of the day with new haircuts and shaves. Our shoes were polished like mirrors. We had inspection of living quarters just before the parade. Everything had to meet military specifications. Then we heard the Drum and Bugle Corps! The performances had to be demoralizing and embarrassing for everyone except those who were educated in music. To those the performances were so laughable that it was difficult to march, stand at attention, and do the other required military actions. (I recalled the *Munich Mountaineers* LP from the party in Atlanta.) We referred to the corps as the Bum and Droogle Corpse.

A Drum and Bugle Corps is well-suited to the musical functions of a military base. There are only bugles (soprano, alto, tenor, and bass) with snare and bass drums. The music is generally very simple, but it can be inspiring if well done. Almost anyone can be trained in a few months to play *some* part in such a musical organization, but good discipline and reasonable preparation are necessary. I found both sorely lacking.

I interviewed the noncommissioned officer in charge of the corps. I also interviewed some members of the corps, asking particularly how they spent their time in that assignment. I found that they had no duties other than rehearsal and performance at the base. Their assigned building was entirely adequate for rehearsal and individual practice. Their equipment was also of good quality, and they had sufficient music for their purpose. Apparently, they spent little time in rehearsal or practice, devoting much time to commercial engagements in the community. This put them into competition with civilian musicians, which was unethical and perhaps illegal.

I ended my study with recommendations, the preferred one being that the corps should be disbanded and its members reassigned to other duties. I assumed that the study was just for my practice and that it would not be implemented. I was wrong! The officer in charge accepted my recommendation, and in a very short time, the corps was gone! That was the first time anyone in the Air Force took my opinion seriously and acted upon it. I heard that the members of the corps were egregiously displeased with my study and recommendations. I was sorry, but the study *was* done properly, and I was convinced that the recommendations were appropriate.

In addition to flying practice in the local area, Basic Training required a considerable amount of navigation practice (cross-country flying). We took trips to El Paso, Texas, and Cocoa Island, Florida (which was renamed Kennedy Center a few years later). Our instructors had us do all the flight planning, file flight plans, attend weather briefings, and any other duties normally associated with cross-country missions. They carefully checked everything we did, making corrections as necessary. During the flights one student always sat in the nose of the plane (the bombardier position in combat), navigating by dead-reckoning and coordinating with the pilot. We were gradually assuming the duties of fully-qualified pilots.

"Solo flying" was really flying with another student but no instructor. We were able to change seats while flying, the pilot in command flying in the left seat while the other student acted as co-pilot. Solo flying tempted some students into shenanigans that were not generally mentioned except as rumors.

One such shenanigan that we heard about was the "bombing" of a large boulder in the panhandle of Texas. Apparently, students would lay a watermelon on the bomb-bay doors, fly to the boulder, and open the bomb-bay doors at the calculated time to drop the "bomb." I heard that the boulder was well stained with watermelon juice, a tribute to the marksmanship of some unknown student pilots.

Another story that spread through our class may or may not be true, but it was so popular that I believed it. If it isn't true it should be!

It seems that two students were returning to Reese after a night "solo" flight. They contacted Reese tower for landing clearance.

"Reese tower, this is [ID] entering traffic for landing."

"[ID], this is Reese tower. I do not have you in sight. Continue approach."

"Uh, roger tower, [ID] entering downwind."

"[ID], this is the tower. I still do not have you in sight. Continue approach."

Somehow, the students had flown to Hobbs, New Mexico (our auxiliary field, which looked superficially similar to Reese but was about seventy-five miles southwest). They were on the downwind leg of Hobbs but in contact with the tower at Reese! Their altitude was much too low, and they touched down briefly in the sand at Hobbs!

The story continues that they were near a lovers' lane where a cadet and his girlfriend were parked in their car. I tried to imagine the conversation in that car as the two occupants heard and saw a B-25 touch down nearby and then roar away, clawing for altitude with full throttles. It is likely that the conversation ended with "Would you like a cigarette?" As the movies of the day show, we smoked cigarettes to mark most truly memorable occasions.

We finished our training and check rides. Suddenly, it was time for graduation—this time, with wings! Those of us who applied would receive commercial licenses, Single and Multi-Engine with Instrument Ratings (worth thousands of dollars if training were done at a civilian school). I applied.

We received our wings, along with typical inspirational speeches, at a Saturday morning parade (minus the Drum and Bugle

Corps). We said goodbye to our classmates and were off to Advanced Training, which for me was Transition to B-47s at McConnell Air Force Base, Wichita, Kansas. (We had been given a choice of several different assignments, one of which was a new space program. The Air Force was to train a carefully selected group of men to go into space aboard a rocket and orbit for an unannounced period of time before returning to earth. We laughed about this plan, saying it was ridiculous and that it would never happen. I never knew anyone who applied for this assignment. Only later did we hear about the actual space flights. Theoretically, some of us might have been involved in those!)

17

The B-47 reminded me of a space ship. It was the largest airplane I had ever seen up close (the B-36 was larger, but I had seen it only at a distance). Its swept wings that drooped when the plane was parked, its six jet engines hanging on pylons beneath the wings, its droppable wing tanks, its large front and rear main landing gear, its tiny outrigger gear beneath each wing, its jaunty canopy, its two menacing tail guns, and its radar dome beneath the crew compartment all bespoke a dignified but deadly killing machine prepared to terrorize anyone who might *think* of attacking the United States. Beneath that highly-polished skin were systems and more systems that transitioning crews had to learn to operate. We had ninety days to accomplish that. Later when I saw the movie *Strategic Air Command* with James Stewart, I could fully appreciate the beauty and complexity of the B-47. (I watch that movie over and over, approximately once each year.)

The B-47 flew with a crew of three: navigator/bombardier, pilot, and aircraft commander. In the aisle, there was a small platform equipped with a safety belt. A fourth person could ride there if necessary. Sometimes the crew chief (a noncommissioned officer) flew to build flying time and to check various systems in flight. At other times a VIP might fly there as a passenger. During transition, I flew in the fourth "seat," since there were only two cockpit seats, and they were occupied by the transitioning aircraft commander (in front) and the instructor (in the rear crew position). It was crowded and cramped, and I hesitate to write about the relief tubes and toilet arrangements! We trained ourselves not to need the latter, but we needed the former almost every flight (eight to twelve hours). This need usually arose just before or just after we consumed our flight lunches.

We wore regular underwear, insulated underwear, and flight suits. We also wore parachute harness that had straps around our legs next to our bodies. With all those layers we needed to be well-endowed in order to neatly manage the relief tube. The lesser-endowed would not need the packet of salt that was included in our flight lunches. (There were no provisions for washing hands.) Not to worry! We were assured that urine was sanitary: it could be used as a disinfectant in an emergency! (An apocryphal story circulated about relief tubes: it seems that a flight instructor was asked by his gullible student what was the purpose of that tube. The instructor replied that it was a microphone of the old type that transmitted sound through the air. It was necessary to hold it tightly against the mouth in order for it to work. The student reportedly tried it several times. We didn't hear about the results.)

Our flight lunches were packed just before time for takeoff. They included regular field rations plus a carton of milk, a small can of tomato juice, and a piece of fried chicken. The lunches always spent some time in the aircraft while we finished the four-hour pre-flight. More time was spent starting engines, taxiing, taking off, climbing, levelling off, and doing one or more of the training exercises scheduled for that mission. By the time we ate the lunches, they had chilled for several hours, and the fried chicken was covered with congealed cooking oil. The rest of the lunch was also cold, but nothing seemed to affect it. We managed to eat without thinking very much about the process. It was simply a means to an end. Flying in the B-47 was undoubtedly better than living in a foxhole, but it couldn't compare to a fine hotel!

Each member of the crew had assigned duties. The aircraft commander was usually qualified to fill any of the three positions on the crew. He generally had many years of experience and thousands of hours flying time in the B-47. Duties specific to his position included operating the automatic pilot, in-flight refueling, selecting fuel tanks to be used in flight using the fuel intake manifold controls (which were in the front crew position only) and initiating radio communications. He was literally in command of the aircraft and responsible for every decision that was made during flight.

The pilot was usually a younger person with much less experience than the aircraft commander. He could be described as an *understudy* in training to become an aircraft commander. He was fully qualified to fly the plane and was required to act as pilot in command for a certain number of hours per month. Duties specific to that position included defense of the aircraft against attacks (he could turn his seat around 180 degrees to accomplish radar-aiming of the two 20mm tail guns), operate the fuel-intake manifold to control weight and balance of fuel on the ground and during aerial refueling, assist the navigator-bombardier with celestial navigation by operating a sextant through a port above the rear cockpit, and assist the aircraft commander with any of the tasks required to plan and execute a flight.

The navigator/bombardier operated all equipment associated with navigation in flight, especially on bomb-runs. Most of this was done with radar, located at the front crew position. Shortly after takeoff the aircraft commander would place the aircraft on automatic pilot, after which the navigator/bombardier was in control of the plane until we completed our mission and were ready to descend and land. Occasionally, one of the two pilots would take the plane off autopilot during the flight and practice *flying*, but we couldn't do it as well as the autopilot. (We were concerned that we might fly so long we would forget how to land, like the famous "gooney-birds" we had seen on television.)

The three crew-members could not see each other while operating the aircraft. This necessitated instant and intuitive coordination. We constantly worked to improve this in the air and in the B-47 simulator. The Air Force also took measures to ensure that members of crews were compatible psychologically.

The B-47 had many shortcomings which were discovered after the plane was placed in service. One of these was duty overload for the crew. We generally accepted the idea that if we had more than fifteen seconds between tasks we had forgotten something and must run a quick recheck. We were totally worn out after each mission, which lasted eight to twelve hours. The Air Force was aware of the plane's shortcomings and was planning the successor to the B-47—the B-52, one of the greatest planes ever designed. Unfortunately, I was never able to fly a B-52. My tour of active duty ended before the opportunity came.

We finished transition rather unceremoniously and departed to our combat-ready base (Lincoln Air Force Base for me). I was the only new pilot to arrive at Lincoln at that time, so it was necessary for me to upgrade to combat-ready status by myself. I had a long list of requirements to accomplish, having the person in charge of each requirement certify that I had completed it. I went to survival training for about two weeks in northern California and to gunnery school in Salinas, Kansas, for several days for practice in the operation of B-47 tail-guns. Along with several other new pilots, I was invited by my friend Lt. Richard Overmann to have dinner at his home in Salinas. Richard's mother prepared a wonderful meal that included slow-cooked roast beef with potatoes, carrots, and onions, one of my favorites.

Gunnery school included actually firing the two 20-mm. cannons found on B-47s. The tail-section of a plane had been mounted on a platform on the ground with the radar connected. We sat in front of the radar screen just as we would in a B-47. A ground crew would launch a small radio-controlled drone and make passes at our guns simulating a fighter attack at altitude. The drone would fly at 180 knots airspeed, the same closing speed that an F-86 would have at altitude. We would lock on to the drone and fire seven-second bursts at it (not steady firing, as that would melt the barrels of our guns). We found out that our guns had been set to miss the drones (for budget reasons), but even so, one or two marksmen actually shot down their targets. When the drones ran out of fuel, their wings would tip up, causing them to stall. A parachute would open, and they would lower harmlessly to the ground. Later, when we were flying practice missions, pilots of F-86s would contact us asking permission to practice attacks against us. We would grant them permission, warm up the radar, and practice locking on and firing at them (of course, all weapons were empty at such times).

When I became combat-ready, it was time to be assigned to a crew. I was invited to dinner with my prospective aircraft commander and navigator-bombardier, Captains Loney and Murphy. We had a good time, but they tended to talk mostly about engineering while my conversation tended toward music. After a time, Captain Loney said, "You *are* an engineer, aren't you?" I explained that I was a violinist, and I noticed they both men developed a rather crestfallen expression. Engineers were quite welcome as crewmembers, but violinists? I explained that one of my degrees, the BME, was bachelor of music education, not mechanical engineering! I was accepted anyway, and I remained on that crew until I had almost finished active duty.

18

Every military pilot has at least one "hairy tale," a flying experience that could have ended in disaster. "And there I was, my engines flamed out and my plane upside down at thirty thousand feet."

I was a member of a lead crew flying B-47 aircraft out of Lincoln AFB, Nebraska (Strategic Air Command). We had a passenger for the flight in question: a public information officer (a sort of news reporter). He was a former student pilot who had been "washed out" of flying training and was serving his remaining tour of duty in his civilian specialty. He had been in England doing research for a story about SAC crew living conditions. I was classified as "pilot," although I was doing co-pilot duties in the rear cockpit. The navigator-bombardier was Captain Murphy, and the aircraft commander was Captain Loney.

One of our missions was called "Reflex." Every crew had an Emergency War Plan (EWP), which we studied continually, and all our training was meant to develop the skills necessary to complete our EWP mission. The United States was not at war, but our work was in a sort of gray area between war and peace. At any moment, the sound of a klaxon horn could signal that we were at war. The Reflex mission consisted of flying to our forward base near London, England, and remaining there on alert for a certain amount of time. At the Reflex base our aircraft were "cocked" (placed on full alert), with H-bombs on board and all fuel, ammunition, and other supplies ready for takeoff on an actual bombing mission. Each crew remained in the UK for at least one week, often more, during which we had at least one practice alert every day. These could be at any time during the day or night, and when we rushed out to the aircraft, we did not know whether we were at war or not until we had started the engines and taxied out for takeoff. Then we would receive a signal that this was a practice alert and that we were to return to our parking space. We were usually very tired when our temporary duty on Reflex was finished and we prepared to return to Lincoln.

We took off at dusk from our Reflex base, already tired. Our crew rest had been insufficient, and we had little food that was nourishing or appetizing. In England, the runway was much closer to the town than it was in Lincoln, and we flew over the picturesque little city at what seemed a marginal altitude and high speed. I always breathed a sigh of relief when we reached a few thousand feet with landing gear and flaps up and at a normal climb speed.

We flew to the west toward the United States doing sunline navigation and other training activities (we seldom simply *flew*). We were notified that our aerial-refueling tanker would not be available, which was not very surprising. It seemed that we missed aerial refueling about 50 percent of the time, often due to maintenance problems on the aging KC-97 tankers. We would be diverting to Goose Bay, Labrador, for ground refueling. We arrived at the Goose after dark.

The weather was rather poor when we parked our B-47 in the refueling area. There was a light rain, cold temperatures near freezing, some wind, and a low ceiling. I was left in charge of refueling while the other two members of the crew went to Operations to file our new flight plan.

Captains Loney and Murphy returned to the plane just after refueling was finished, and we were ready to take off. Captain Loney had a cheeseburger and a stalk of celery that he had managed to find, and he broke off a bite of each for me. This was the only food I had in about six hours, and I felt a bit queasy.

We were in a formation of six B-47s. "Formation" was the word we used, but it did not have the meaning that it had in World War II! If we were able to see the other planes, we were close enough together, but we did take off as a group at about two-minute intervals. Our plane was second in order of takeoff: in the first the aircraft commander was Captain Loney's former AC. As we prepared to start engines, there was considerable chatter on the radio. Several crew members from the other planes suggested that it was a spooky night and that we would do well to stay and continue our trip the next morning. For some reason, no person in authority issued such a command. Perhaps we were still in "war-play" mode: we certainly would not stay overnight under these conditions if we were at war!

We taxied out for takeoff. The first plane took the active runway, and we took its place, stopping on the taxiway just short of the runway and at an angle. The first plane began its takeoff run.

At about the time the first plane should leave the runway, I saw a brilliant blue flash of light, which reminded me of the flashbulb in use at the time for photography. I turned toward the flash and saw about one mile of yellow flames beginning approximately at the end of the runway and extending out into Goose Bay. I heard at least one crew member say on the radio, "There has been an actual crash." No answer came from the control tower, possibly because the low, ragged clouds hid the flames.

Captain Loney taxied our plane onto the active runway. He went through the normal procedure, holding the brakes and running the engines up to 100 percent power. I knew that he was having an attack of nerves when I felt the brakes shake and the aircraft try to creep during the run-up. I helped him hold the brakes until time to release them and begin the takeoff roll.

Takeoff was normal, and the landing gear came up at the correct time. As our speed reached 195 knots, I began to retract flaps. Normal climb attitude was established, and our speed was 310 knots. We were in and out of the ragged clouds almost immediately upon leaving the runway. I was intently watching the instruments as Captain Loney was also monitoring instruments and looking outside the aircraft.

At 1,200 feet altitude, we suddenly began to descend. Captain Murphy (in the crew station forward of the cockpit) screamed, "We're descending!" several times. Although our climbing attitude did not change, our rate of climb/descent changed to one thousand feet per minute downward! We were about one minute from crashing.

Several times in my life I have felt that I was acting automatically, almost as if I were outside my body watching my actions. This was one of those times. Without thought or hesitation, I took control of the aircraft. The thought crossed my mind, *If we crash, I want it to be tail-low and slow.*

My right hand automatically pushed the throttles full forward as if I were trying to bend them past the stops. My left hand smoothly pulled the yoke back to establish a nose-high attitude. As soon as we passed through 195 knots airspeed, I started the flaps down.

The B-47 was slow to react compared to a fighter or trainer aircraft. It was heavy, and it was not designed for low-level aerobatics. It seemed to take ages for the control inputs I had initiated to take effect. I watched the instruments as our altitude went to one hundred feet, still descending. I remembered sessions in the flight simulator when so many emergency conditions had been added that the airplane must inevitably crash, accompanied by a shaking of the seat and the sound of the buzzer. I remember thinking, *We'll hear the buzzer any time now.*

At approximately one hundred feet indicated altitude, our plane stopped descending and began climbing. Perhaps we were in ground effect. I know that we descended for only a few seconds from the time Captain Murphy screamed until I answered calmly (!), "It's all right, Murph. I helped him a little bit." I sounded almost like an *instructor*, which was a great surprise to me.

I almost could not believe what had happened. I tried to figure out why I had been able to do what I did with hardly any loss of composure. One factor, I am sure, was the excellent training given by our flight instructors. Only a few days before this Reflex flight, I had my annual instrument flying exam. One of our best squadron pilots (a major whose name I can't remember), who was also an instructor pilot, had examined me in an actual B-47 flight. He gave a thorough exam that was unusual in that it not only found my weaknesses and attempted to correct them: it also built my confidence.

As soon as we reached cruising altitude, Captain Loney ordered us to take a "go" pill, a large white pill that stimulated the body like strong coffee and made us feel that we had been sleeping for

119

about eight hours. I remember how beautiful the night looked, with a bright moon, millions of stars, and lovely clouds in a squall line that extended for many miles and reminded me of the columns in the Parthenon.

When we arrived at Lincoln, a number of my friends met us at the plane. They thought that I was in the plane that crashed and that I had been killed. We found out that the plane in front of us had hit terrific wind shear just after takeoff, had not made emergency corrections, and had crashed on the ice of Goose Bay. The navigator (in the nose of the plane) had been killed by the impact, estimated at six hundred miles per hour. The pilot (in the back seat) had drowned after the plane melted through the ice, and the aircraft commander had been found walking on the ice near the crash site. He had somehow been thrown from the plane as it broke up. His only injury was a slipped disc in his spine.

Maintenance crews discovered that our plane had been damaged, presumably by excessive "G" forces in the pullout from its sudden descent. We had lost the nose cone from one of our engines, and the drag chute was also gone, never to be recovered. (The drag chute is a large parachute contained in a special compartment in the tail of the plane. When deployed upon landing, it slows the aircraft considerably, saving wear on the brakes. It is attached to the airframe by a metal link that will break at airspeeds above 160 knots. It is possible that our tail scraped the ice during the descent, causing our chute to deploy, and the excessive speed caused it to shear.) We had already discovered that we also lost the "artificial feel," which was also located in the tail.

The B-47 ailerons, elevator, and rudder were connected to the flight controls by cables in a manner similar to those connections in small aircraft such as the popular Piper Cub. The difference was that in the B-47 the control surfaces were so large that it was difficult to move the cockpit controls without a power assist (similar to power steering on a car). However, the power assist was so powerful that it made it possible to move the control surface *too* rapidly, possibly causing damage to the control surfaces. The solution was artificial feel, a system that allowed ram air near the vertical stabilizer to enter a sensing device that controlled a computer that calculated how the cockpit controls should feel at various airspeeds. Because of the danger of damage to control surfaces, loss of artificial feel was classified as an emergency. As we neared Lincoln AFB, Captain Loney declared an emergency landing, which was accomplished without further incident.

Strategic Air Command was considerably agitated by the crash of one of *our* planes and the emergency measures made necessary by others. Generals, colonels, and others descended upon Lincoln AFB in large numbers, seeking information which might be useful in preventing similar occurrences. I was asked to testify in front of a great collection of "brass." I don't know whether my testimony had any effect upon policy, but I did give an opinion to my aircraft commander after he and our navigator-bombardier congratulated me upon my actions: "Now that we've proven that we *can* do this, let's not do it any more unless we're at war."

19

I made so many trips to England that I lost count of them. It seems that every time we landed in Lincoln, Nebraska, someone met me at the plane and told me to get ready as rapidly as possible: I was going back to England. At some point in the confusion, I convinced Teena that we should be married as soon as possible. I had only a few months of active duty left, and I rationalized that that much *military wife* experience might be good for Teena. I was surprised but delighted when she agreed!

Patricia Kent, Teena's sister, took the major responsibility for our wedding plans, assisted eventually by members of both families and many members of the community. In some ways, I was fortunate to be on active duty in the Air Force, often flying to Europe and spending weeks there, so I didn't have to help with the plans.

Originally, the wedding was to be simple, with twenty family members present. As more and more ideas developed, the numbers expanded so that approximately one hundred attended the ceremony (limited by the size of Beck Chapel, which was supposed to hold seventy-five). No one knew how many attended the reception, but I would guess three hundred. It was held on the rooftop terrace of the IU Memorial Union, a beautiful location for such a gathering. Donald Neal, my first violin teacher, played at the reception accompanied by piano. For at least six months, we planned the wedding with the date set: August 10, 1958. For a time, the Air Force seemed to have other ideas, even though I had applied for a ten-day leave and had received approval.

Several weeks before our scheduled wedding, there was an international crisis in Lebanon. The crisis was small at first, but it gradually expanded to become very large. The United States was nearly at war! Strategic Air Command was on full alert, progressing by stages to the point where we were told that the next thing we might hear would be the klaxon horn announcing that we were at war and that we were to race out to our planes and fly our missions. We had already passed the stage when we turned in everything on our persons that might serve to identify us except our name tags (in case we were shot down and captured). In a meeting with my aircraft commander and the squadron commander, I was told that I had three possibilities concerning my wedding: (1) The Air Force would fly me in a jet trainer to Indiana where I could be married and flown back to Lincoln immediately. (2) The Air Force would fly my bride to Lincoln where we could be married in the chapel, and she would be flown back to Indiana immediately. (3) The crisis could end, and I could proceed with my leave and wedding plans.

The crisis continued for several weeks, during which all normal activities on the base were suspended. We were in alert mode, which meant that we spent most of the day preparing for and waiting for the klaxon horn to sound. Married officers were allowed to bring their wives and children on base as visitors, and they spent most of their time in the Officers' Club. The rest of us spent time in the barracks. I took my violin to an empty room and practiced, dressed in a flight suit and carrying a snub-nosed pistol in a shoulder holster as required. I tried to move as far away from other crew members as possible, but some of them would drop in as I practiced. They would lean against the wall and sit on their heels, sometimes interrupting me to make comments or ask questions. I was often surprised at the amount of interest they had in music and how informed they were. After a few days, we all became acclimated to the situation and began to assume that the crisis was being settled, and that war was not likely. Then one night, someone at SAC Headquarters in Omaha decided to call a practice alert.

We had been told that there would be no practice alerts during the crisis. If we heard the klaxon, we were at war; if we heard a siren, the Russians had already launched missiles toward Lincoln, and we wouldn't have time to get to our planes and take off. Under those circumstances, we were advised to get in our cars and drive as fast as possible away from the base. "You won't get anywhere, but it will give you something to do while waiting for the big, blue light!"

Practice alerts were signaled by the klaxon, the same horn that was to signal the beginning of war. When the klaxon sounded, immediate pandemonium struck. Officers' wives and children were crying as they struggled to get to crew members for a last hug. Pilots and crewmembers were in a panic, collecting cases and materials necessary for their missions. One young navigator was in the shower when the klaxon sounded. Clad only in soapsuds, he dashed out of the shower, grabbed his flight bag in one hand and his boots and flight suit in the other, and fought his way through the crowd of hysterical wives, children, and crew members on the way to his plane. When we arrived at our planes, we were told that regardless of previous orders, this was a practice alert and we were to return to our quarters. We followed those directions, even though doing so was a technical violation of orders, and in case of war, this was exactly what the enemy might do to prevent our taking off.

After a few days, I was again summoned to a meeting where I was told that the crisis was over, and I could continue with wedding plans. I drove to Bloomington, Indiana, where I had a few days left as a single man. I spent the greater part of those days and nights with my parents in the home where I grew up. The rest of the time I was with Teena and her family.

On August 10, our wedding day, I slept fairly late, had a good breakfast, and began preparing for the wedding. Even with all the months of preparation for our wedding, I was keenly aware that this was my *last day* as a single man. Everything would seem different beginning tomorrow.

As I had often done while growing up, I took my bath in the creek. The creek bed consisted of large sandstones, naturally hollowed out to the size of a bathtub, and the continuous stream of sparkling water was refreshing. There was no need to be concerned with clothing as the trees offered complete privacy.

After my leisurely bath, I dressed in my tux with a white dinner jacket. I had not worn this outfit since joining the Air Force, so I was surprised that it was so large! The coat seemed at least two inches too large, and I thought it looked terrible, but it was too late to do anything about it. I drove to Beck Chapel for the afternoon wedding, noting that it was one of the hottest days in my experience.

Beck Chapel is a jewel of architecture located near the Memorial Union Building on the IU campus. It is an exact replica of a fourteenth-century chapel located in France, built of Indiana limestone with a slate roof. It departs from the model only in the sense that it has modern electric lighting, plumbing, and air-conditioning. Members of the IU community are allowed to schedule appropriate events there, but it is not used for regular services by any denomination. In 1958, there was a small electronic organ in the chapel. That has since been replaced by a wonderful small pipe organ, a "tracker," which is perfectly suited to its purpose. Further adding to the authenticity of the setting and, bridging the cultural gap between medieval France and modern Indiana, there is a small cemetery adjoining the chapel. The cemetery is enclosed inside a stone wall with an ornamental gate at the entrance. The cemetery was already there when the IU campus was begun, and there is an agreement that it will never be disturbed.

The chapel was beautifully decorated for our wedding. When I arrived, several friends had already been seated and more were milling about inside and outside. The carillon in the tower of the Student Building was playing familiar hymns, including my favorite "Beneath the Cross of Jesus" and Teena's favorite, "Shepherd, Show Me How to Go." I don't know exactly how this was managed, but our folks knew practically everyone on campus including (I suppose) the carillon player.

The organ prelude was performed by Professor Wolfgang Vocano, the IU opera conductor, who was also the organist of The Christian Science Church. Teena's father, tenor Otis O. Patton, sang Grieg's "Ich Liebe Dich." Then it was time for the processional.

Many movies have attempted portrayals of bridegrooms, and everyone has an idea how they must feel, but I had never imagined feeling as I did when I heard the beginning of the "Wedding March" and saw Teena marching with her father down the aisle toward me. I felt a confusion of almost every possible emotion, which I will not attempt to describe for fear of becoming maudlin. Perhaps the memory of my recent military experiences combined with the experience of the moment caused my emotional machinery to shut down. I could think only how dry my throat felt and how much I would pay for a glass of cold orange juice!

Somehow we progressed through the ceremony to the point where we exchanged vows. Teena managed these very well. I repeated the vows, but my voice was so weak it seemed inaudible. (We have a recording of the wedding, and I can barely be heard. Colonel King, my professor of Air Science and Tactics and a friend of the Patton family said that I put on a "good act." Whatever it was, it definitely was no act!). In our wedding photos, I look almost normal, although very skinny in my ill-fitting coat. I was also almost hairless because pilots usually had very short haircuts. I seemed to have appropriate facial expressions, mostly smiling, but I do not notice myself: the vision of Teena commands the attention of anyone looking at our pictures.

As we left the chapel, someone handed me a telegram. It was from my crew at Lincoln Air Force Base. It congratulated me and announced that we would have a "stand-board exam" on Monday, just two days away! Goodbye, Colorado honeymoon.

We had planned for a week-long honeymoon in Colorado, but we had to cancel those plans and go immediately to our little rented house at 3257 Hitchcock Street in Lincoln, Nebraska.

20

Teena and I rented a new little frame rancher at 3257 Hitchcock Street in Lincoln. It was pink with white trim, and it stood near another just like it except that it was lime green and white. There were two bedrooms, a bath, kitchen, and dining area, all small. The main charm of the house was that it was brand-new (and clean). Both houses were situated on lots in a new subdivision, which at that time, had no other houses. It was a fine first home for newlyweds, and it cost exactly the amount of my housing allowance. (The citizens of Lincoln knew Air Force personnel quite well, including our income and allowances.) We were within walking distance of a shopping center that included a Piggly-Wiggly supermarket.

Soon after we moved into our little pink house, the weather became cooler as autumn began. One morning, we turned our gas furnace on, but it didn't start immediately. We had breakfast, and I prepared to leave for the air base. I gave Teena a goodbye kiss just as the furnace started. From all the registers came a puff of smoke that smelled of burnt paint. At first we were rather alarmed, but then we figured out what was going on with the new furnace, duct-work, and registers. We agreed that we were one hot couple!

Most of our furniture in the pink house was given to us by Teena's parents. It was red maple, and it was their first furniture when they were married. They had it refurbished for us until it looked new, and it was very comfortable. We had a couch and chair, a small dinette with four chairs, and several tables. Teena and I rented a small upright piano. We purchased a Hollywood bed along with towels, curtains, sheets, and other bedding. We also purchased glasses, dishes, and tableware. We used a coin laundry, and our refrigerator came with the house. We were quite comfortable, and we were both glad that we were married six months before my scheduled release from active Air Force duty.

"Stand-board" is an abbreviation for Standardization Board Exam, one of the requirements of Strategic Air Command in 1958. A few days after our wedding, I was in front of the Board at Lincoln Air Force Base reciting my duties in the event our crew was ordered to execute its Emergency War Plan. We were expected to be prepared to do our part even if all our paperwork became unavailable. This required memorization of routes, radio frequencies, timing, altitudes, and other details of the mission beginning with our preflight inspection and ending with the release of our weapon. Each crew was tested as a unit so we could recite actions in the order we would perform them, almost like a theatrical production. The Board consisted of one or more officers from SAC Headquarters in Omaha. "Stand-Boards" were very important, and everyone made supreme efforts to do well on them.

Apparently, officers assigned to examine crews on stand-boards made considerable efforts to study the crews being examined. I thought of myself as an inconsequential, nearly invisible first lieutenant just trying to survive and fulfill my duties. I was quite surprised when the major general in charge of the examination departed from the script, so to speak, and asked, "How is the violin coming along?" I hadn't realized that people could hear me as I practiced in an empty barracks room. I already knew that a number of them had visited the room as I practiced.

Teena and I quickly settled into the routine of Air Force living, generally following a work schedule similar to that of a regular job. Interruptions could come at any time in the form of alerts or special training trips, but these were rather few and easily managed. We soon learned not to accept social engagements at any time day or night without an understanding that we might have to cancel them.

Although the time schedule was similar to that of a regular job, few days in our squadron were routine. Since I was a member of a combat-ready crew, our weekly schedule was divided into three parts:

planning missions, flying missions, and debriefing missions. To fill any time left between these activities, all of us had extra duties. I was weight and balance officer for the squadron. I was also (automobile) driving safety officer.

In planning our missions, we had to know which training objectives needed to be completed by our crew within a specified time. I had to fire our two tail-guns (20-mm cannons) at least once every six months, which involved flight-planning to arrive over a specified target without wasting time getting there. We had to complete a certain number of navigation "legs" on each flight, a certain number of radar bomb runs, in-flight refueling, simulated actual bomb-drops using a twenty-five-pound bomb with ballistics similar to those of our assigned weapon, and other requirements. One of the more interesting requirements was the "pop-up" mission.

Most military aircraft are designed for a specific mission, but after the planes become combat-ready, new missions are often discovered or invented. "Pop-up" was one of those for the B-47.

Nuclear weapons grew in size and in nuclear yield quickly after the first fission weapons were put into use (Hiroshima and Nagasaki). Fusion weapons (hydrogen bombs) were soon invented. These were the current weapons when I became combat-ready.

"H" bombs, as they were called, could make a very large, glass-lined hole in the earth. In fact, the explosion was so large there was some danger that the plane that dropped the bomb could not escape the circle of destruction. "Pop-up" was invented to overcome this difficulty.

The "pop-up" mission began several hundred miles from the target. We would establish the plane at a *maximum* altitude of 300 feet above terrain and an airspeed of 310 knots indicated (approximately 355 miles per hour). Navigation was done by visual reference to the ground and to marked maps. Usually we flew these missions in Wisconsin.

The route was generally rural, but there were small towns on the way. There were also television towers, which were higher than our altitude. Sometimes I felt that if we extended our landing gear we would be on the ground. By the time we identified a feature of terrain, it was often impossible to avoid flying over it because of our speed. Our sound traveled only slightly ahead of us, so we could see people on the ground suddenly jerk their heads back to get a glimpse of us as we flew over. (The B-47 made a terrifying sound in the configuration necessary to this mission.) We sometimes flew over school playgrounds full of children, and we saw whole groups do the head-jerk. We could also see the terror in their eyes.

There were many turkey farms along the routes chosen for this mission. The turkeys were large, white birds bred for commercial sale. We would see hundreds, perhaps thousands of these great birds as they fled in panicky groups until they came to a fence. At that point, they would pile up in huge numbers, smothering those in the lower layers. The US government received large bills to pay for damages. I am also sure that many complaints were received about the annoyance caused by "joy-riding jet jockeys."

When we arrived at a specified place in our route, we advanced throttles to 100 percent power, maintained our air speed and accepted the resulting rate of climb. We would assume a steep-climbing attitude: our rate-of-climb instruments would be pegged at maximum.

At eighteen thousand feet altitude, we would simulate releasing our weapon (we never did this with actual weapons on board, but radar could calculate the trajectory our bomb would take in actual conditions). The bomb was designed to continue climbing toward the target and gradually begin to descend. A parachute in the tail of the bomb would slow its descent until it reached a designated altitude. Meanwhile, we would be escaping, at least in theory.

After releasing the bomb (simulated or actual) we would do a sort of Immelman maneuver, a wingover combined with a steep turn away from the target. We would lower the nose and dive steeply to lose altitude as quickly as possible. When we reached three hundred feet maximum, we would continue until time to begin another assigned objective or return to base.

After such a mission, I would arrive at our pink house rather tired. My bride would greet me with a kiss and ask what I did that day. My answer would be something like, "Oh, we flew a mission mostly in Wisconsin."

She would say something like, "I hope you didn't fly very high," to which I would answer, "Oh no, not very. What are we having for dinner?"

The B-47 consumed an impressive amount of fuel doing the pop-up mission. The plane was designed to fly in level flight at a constant cruising speed above twenty-five thousand feet. Also, the wings showed signs of weakness in this mission. They were modified by placing rows of heavy rivets near the wing roots. The protruding rivets severely damaged the appearance of the plane, but that didn't seem to matter. The B-52 was on the horizon as a replacement for the ageing B-47.

Sometimes after roll call (7:30 a.m.), we would be told that our crew had no scheduled duties for the day. This meant that we could catch up with our extra duties. One day, I decided to spend my time with weight and balance.

The B-47 required careful attention to weight and balance. Often called "the flying fuel tank," it could hold almost its weight in JP-4 fuel in three main tanks and two auxiliary wing-tip tanks (that could be dropped in flight). After a B-47 was sent to maintenance, it was weighed and its balance (center of gravity) rechecked. Aircrews used the new numbers in flight-planning to calculate setting the trim for takeoff and for planning the use of available runway. As weight and balance officer, my duty was to keep accurate and up-to-date records for the use of the squadron.

I began by calling maintenance.

R-r-r-ing! Answer: "Hello, this is maintenance, Sergeant H—speaking."

"Hello, this is Lieutenant Richardson, 344th. I'm calling to get the weight and balance on B-47 number 791. Could you give me that, please?"

"Wal now, Lieutenant, the man in charge of that is on temporary duty in Florida and won't be back until next week. Try calling Sergeant L—."

This basic message was repeated several times with different phone numbers and names. Finally one person gave me a number with the comment "He's the man in charge. If he doesn't know the weight and balance, no one does."

I dialed the number. It was my other phone!

My other extra duty was squadron driving safety officer. The need for such a position might be questioned until one examined the auto driving skills on our base: we had more casualties driving cars than flying planes during my assignment there! (Perhaps I should say flying cars and driving planes?)

My duty was to remind everyone in the squadron of the need for safe driving. My method was to create charts with graphs showing behavioral trends related to safety. We had a goodly supply of poster board, overlay plastic sheets in striking colors, and a variety of colored plastic tape in various widths. I would create beautiful charts to decorate our assembly room. I am sorry to record that the size and prominence of my charts was inversely proportional to the amount of useful information on them, but I did not hear any complaints. Perhaps this was because everyone else was also creating charts relative to *their* extra duties. All of us wanted our charts to be impressive.

Our base commander provided the other half of the driving safety effort. He scheduled his own "traffic court," which he held at 7:30 a.m. on Saturdays in his office. Invited guests included everyone who had a traffic violation during the preceding week along with everyone in the chain of command up to the base commander. Thus an airman third class would be accompanied by his sergeant, captain, major, and lieutenant colonel, almost none of whom would be enthusiastic about the invitation. Multiply this by the number of traffic violators in a given week and there could be an impressive number of guests to be upbraided, admonished, cajoled, "chewed out." Other more colorful expressions described the activities upon these occasions, but I was not convinced that the "traffic court" achieved its purpose.

All young officers that I knew received almost constant encouragement to remain in the Air Force as a career. I could easily understand why this was done, but I had already decided to continue a musical career after serving my "hitch." Teena and I enjoyed our new life in the service, remaining in the little pink house until my release from active duty.

21

Teena and I arrived in Nashville, Tennessee, full of excitement in early February 1959, the day after my release from active duty as a pilot in the Air Force. I had requested and received an early release from the USAF because there were more pilots in my Strategic Air Command squadron than there were crew slots available. Quite a few of the surplus pilots were career men, and being unassigned did not help careers. I was convinced that I could make a better contribution to society by teaching at David Lipscomb College than by remaining another six months in the Air Force. The offer of a faculty position at DLC had surprised me since I held only two bachelor's degrees (not the usual master's degree required in college teaching). I was familiar with colleges and universities only through my education at Indiana University, and I thought all colleges and universities were approximately the same. One major difference was that DLC was sponsored by members of our church, which I thought was ideal.

Our first project was to find an apartment. The College invited us to live for a few days in faculty housing, which was in the lower floor of the student dormitory. At first I was embarrassed to ask for a key to our rooms, since DLC was a Christian college, and I couldn't imagine anyone disturbing our few belongings. That was a large mistake: during our first night at the school, police arrested twelve students in the dormitory for operating a crime ring at the school. The students would shoplift in local department stores and sell stolen goods from their rooms. (Rumor had it that fine men's clothing was available at very low prices.) We quickly found a small apartment in a duplex belonging to Mr. and Mrs. Maxwell. The duplex was very near Pat Boone's childhood home. Pat Boone was at the height of his popularity at that time.

As an Air Force first lieutenant, my pay was approximately $7,500 per year plus allowances and flight pay. This was regarded as very good in 1959. At DLC, my faculty pay was $3,600. Per year. I told President Pullias that I didn't see how we could live on that amount, and he predicted (promised?) that if I would do the work assigned me, I would never be at a loss for money. This prediction came true in a surprising way, following several months of financial struggling. (I was in the first violin section of the Nashville Symphony, which paid almost nothing. Sometimes I had to sell our soda bottles in order to pay to park the car during rehearsals or performances.)

My first major performance at DLC was sponsored by the Lipscomb Library Hour. We planned to introduce our new string/orchestra program with a concert featuring all four string instruments (violin, viola, cello, and string bass) with piano performing the Schubert *Trout Quintet.* Since that composition is about forty-five minutes in length, we decided not to add other selections to the program. After the performance in the auditorium, there would be light refreshments in the library and a display of string instruments. I contacted William Moennig and Son in Philadelphia, a highly respected old firm where I had purchased violins for several years. Bill Moennig III agreed to send me a fantastic display of instruments along with the parts of a violin beginning with plain wood and continuing in stages through a completed violin "in the white" (not varnished). He also included an example of all the tools used in the various stages of violin-making. He sent the *Vicomte de la Taille* Stradivarius violin, the Guarnerius del Gesu violin played by Michael Rabin in the movie *Intermezzo,* and a wonderful Gagliano cello once owned by Queen Victoria. The shipment from Mr. Moennig filled two large shipping crates, and the college received the display free of charge! I practiced for about two weeks, alternating between the Stradivarius and the Guarnerius until I decided to perform on the Stradivarius. (It was for sale, priced at $20,000. My mother-in-law of six months offered to buy the violin for me and allow me to repay her at any convenient time, but I didn't accept. I believed that I could buy the violin whenever I wished. What I didn't expect happened, of course: the violin multiplied in value immediately and would now cost millions if it could be purchased at all.)

Our librarian and her staff assembled many photographs and articles describing the history of the violin family. They arranged the materials attractively so that guests could stroll around looking at the displays while partaking of truly delicious food. We had an armed guard present to protect the display, which at the time was probably worth at least one hundred thousand dollars. I couldn't equate the instruments with monetary value: they were priceless, and I realized that no human could actually *own* them! We are mere stewards entrusted with the task of preserving great works of art for future generations.

The concert went as well as it possibly could. Our quintet (composed of myself with members of the Nashville Symphony and our faculty pianist) played very well. We undoubtedly were inspired by the magnificent instruments and the large, attentive audience. Present in the audience were several "country" fiddlers who evidently thought that they would be invited to perform: they brought their fiddles and asked me to look at them during the social hour at the library!

Critics from the Nashville newspapers were very kind about the performance. This was my first experience with public criticism as an individual, although our orchestral performances at Indiana University had been covered many times in local and national publications.

The Schubert performance and library experience were welcome respites from the constant struggle to earn enough money for my family. One day, I met the dean on campus. Always friendly and helpful, he asked me how I was doing. I answered him sincerely: "I don't have any problems that money couldn't solve." I had been taught that material wealth was unimportant, and that people should lay up treasure in heaven "where moth and rust do not corrupt"... I felt that material problems would be solved automatically in order to allow people to accomplish spiritual work. The dean's explosive laughter in answer to my comment suggested to me that he had experienced similar problems!

At about 11:00 p.m., one rainy night, our fortunes changed. I received a phone call from Lillian Hunt, principal second violin of the Symphony and contractor for several recording companies. She asked me if I would like to make a recording. Assuming that she meant for me to record some of the music I had recently performed in recitals, I said, "Yes!" She gave me the location and time of the session, and I asked what music to bring. "Never mind," she said, "we'll furnish the music."

My first session was with a singer I had never heard of named Roy Orbison. It was the worst music I had ever heard or imagined. One of the first tunes was called *Only the Lonely*. When the session was finished, I asked Mrs. Hunt not to call me again. "That's all right," she replied. "For the price we're paying, we can get anyone we want." I discussed the music with some of the other string players, and they were equally appalled. We didn't know how to classify it, but later it came to be called "rock and roll" or just "rock." I was amazed a few weeks later to hear our session almost everywhere I went. *Only the Lonely* sold millions of copies, and it is still selling. I often receive a paycheck for "new use" of this tune in a movie soundtrack (*"Dum, dum, dum, dum, dee doo-ah"*).

A few weeks later, Mrs. Hunt called again and asked me to try another session. She promised that this one would be more musical and more pleasant, so I accepted.

The session was in the old RCA Studio, a rather squat brick building in the middle of a muddy parking lot. I arrived early, and there was only one other person present. We struck up a conversation for a few minutes, and I asked whose session this was. He answered "mine." I then asked who he was, and he answered, "Eddy Arnold"! That session *was* much more pleasant and more musical than my first recording session. I began accepting recording dates routinely after that, and eventually was in the studio orchestra for about two thousand songs, many of them selling more than a million copies. My recording engagements were so numerous they began to threaten my primary purposes in Nashville. (We were known as "the Nashville sound.") Some of the singers who recorded with us were Brenda Lee, Marty Robbins, Porter Wagner, Dolly Parton, Burl Ives, Connie

Frances, Ray Price, Johnnie Ray, Johnnie Horton, Jim Reeves, Patsy Cline, and Ray Charles. Featured instrumentalists included Chet Atkins (guitar), Floyd Cramer (piano), Bill Pursell (piano), and Boots Randolph (saxophone). There were many others whose names I can't remember now.

Representative of the Nashville scene at that time was Boots Randolph. A young high-school band director from New Albany, Indiana, Boots played his first recording session on soprano sax. His playing was very expressive, very musical, and in tune (unusual for that instrument). He was immediately accepted in the group, and he appeared regularly for sessions, playing soprano, alto, and tenor sax. One night (on a Brenda Lee session), Boots must have felt disgusted. He walked over into the corner of the studio and played a crude phrase that must have been the equivalent of swearing on saxophone. The engineer heard it in the control room and came running out. "What was that?" he yelled. Boots didn't seem to have an answer to the question, but the engineer insisted that he improvise a piece of music based on the phrase. *Yakety Sax* was born. It has been so popular that it's safe to bet that almost everyone in the world has heard it.

Another serendipitous example happened in a session with Grady Martin, guitarist. Without his awareness of it, a resistor burned out in his amplifier. (Amplifiers were of the highest quality available, and a very fine microphone was placed as close to the speaker as possible. Volume levels were very low, almost inaudible during recording.) During playback, the guitar sounded fuzzy, as though it was distorting from excessive volume. The engineers were fascinated with the sound, and they investigated to discover what caused it. They devised a small plug-in board with a resistor that would allow "the fuzz" as they called it to be added as the guitarist chose, and the *fuzz* was born! Many hit records were the result of the fuzz, and many stomp boxes were invented to distort the sound of the guitar to fit the demands of the musical style.

Two backup vocal groups who did most of the work at that time were the Anita Kerr Singers and the Jordanaires. Anita Kerr also did many instrumental arrangements. She had never written for strings, but she learned quickly and wrote very musical arrangements, which we enjoyed playing. I admired her work so much that I asked her to write an arrangement for the Lipscomb Strings. She said she would write it, but she couldn't charge me for it because she had already earned so much money that year that practically all her new income would go for taxes. I insisted upon paying her something for the arrangement, so she accepted $25. I still have the arrangement (*Autumn Leaves*) in her handwriting (pencil!), and I suspect it might be worth more than I paid for it.

Backup vocal groups were quite versatile. Sometimes individual members were called upon to sing the solo part for a "take" to try out the arrangement or the microphone settings. They were quite capable of performing in the style of the featured artist, and I thought they did just as well or sometimes better. There was never any indication of jealousy or competition.

One day, I arrived at RCA just a few minutes early (as usual). The session before ours was Elvis Presley, and he was still recording as I arrived. (Elvis used Hollywood strings as needed, and we were never engaged for his sessions.) There was a small audience gathered outside the glass-walled studio, showing their enthusiasm at every opportunity. The Anita Kerr singers (all female voices) were backing him, and the session ran about an hour longer than scheduled. When we finally were admitted to the studio, Elvis had left and the Anita Kerr singers were still there, laughing and quietly joking. I asked what was going on, and one of the singers said that at the beginning of the session Elvis smelled so bad the singers couldn't sing because they were gagging! The session had to be delayed while Elvis went to his hotel for a bath. (He had been on the road for twelve days and had not removed his clothing, including his shoes, during that time.)

The Nashville years were filled with very hard work. I was completing my master's degree at Indiana University during summers, studying violin with Daniel Guilet and chamber music with members of the Beaux Arts Trio, especially cellist Bernard Greenhouse. I also continued playing in the Nashville Symphony, teaching full-time at DLC (which involved founding and conducting the college-community orchestra), performing chamber music and solo recitals in the community, recording in the studios, and helping Teena to care for our three young children, all of whom were born during that time. Ernest Todd was born in 1959, Patricia Beth in 1961, and Edward Scott in 1963.

I heard that Joseph Gingold was teaching at IU during the winter, and I wanted to study with him if possible. I called him, and he kindly scheduled a lesson for me on a Sunday afternoon! When I arrived, he greeted me with casual friendliness and asked what music I was studying. I told him I was preparing for my master of music recital, which could take place in any of the three summers I planned to study at IU. He asked me to begin with a scale of my choice. I chose F major. Thus began one of the most productive lessons I have ever experienced.

Mr. Gingold possessed a vast repertoire of music and technical studies in addition to teaching techniques that enabled him to analyze performance difficulties and recommend ways to overcome them. He was unusually sensitive to the personality of the student: his goal was to be helpful in the mutual quest to master violin performance. He seemed to favor Paganini Caprices, and he asked me to play sections of them. I had not practiced Paganini in preparation for that lesson, and I said several times that I couldn't play what he had requested. His answer was, "I'll bet you a dime that you will be playing this section within five minutes"! Amazingly, I was! I felt that if I could study regularly with him, I could improve greatly as a violinist, and I asked him to call me anytime he could schedule a lesson. He said that was very nice, but he already had a waiting list of eighty-three students, the most distant one living in Hollywood, California.

Our lesson lasted two and one-half hours when we were interrupted by a telephone call from Mrs. Gingold. She asked him whether he planned to ever come home. It was their wedding anniversary!

I was required to remain in the Air Force Reserve for seven years (Universal Military Training) after active duty. I was told that I could be recalled, assigned to a B-47 crew, and sent on a bombing mission with little advance notice. The Cuban Missile Crisis was one occasion when I expected to be called (but it didn't happen). I remember asking myself what I would do if we were notified that a Soviet missile was on its way and we had fifteen minutes left to live. I decided that we could gather our little family around us and listen to some great music, either a Bach *Cantata* or a Mozart *Mass*.

The atmosphere in the recording studios could be the subject of many books. Many of the players didn't trust banks, so they carried large amounts of cash with them. Their wallets were so full of bills that they couldn't be folded: they were wedge-shaped. One person showed me his wallet filled with several thousand-dollar bills, more five-hundred-dollar bills, still more one-hundred-dollar bills, and so forth. Their cash was on display frequently as they played poker games during sessions while the engineers did playbacks. It was not unusual to see thousands of dollars on the table along with the poker hands while we did another "take." I never heard of any dishonest behavior in that situation.

One day, Bob Moore, the bass player, came back from lunch with the news that he had bought a twin-engine Piper airplane during the break. Many of the Nashville musicians were interested in private flying, and a few of them were tragically killed in aircraft accidents while I was in Nashville. There was a tendency to fly into conditions that were too advanced for their training and experience.

One of the star singers owned a new home in the valley east of Nashville. He liked to hold rehearsals at his home at all hours, and the music was often very loud. A close neighbor complained several times. At some point, the singer asked the neighbor, "How much is your house worth?"

The neighbor answered, "Fifty-six thousand dollars." The singer pulled out his wallet and counted fifty-six-thousand-dollar bills. He handed them to his neighbor and said "now get out," which the neighbor did. This kind of financial dealing led to some legal problems and some problems with the IRS.

About two years after we moved to Nashville, we were able to purchase a house. We found one in a good area, even though traffic was rather busy and fast on Woodmont Avenue where it was located. The price was $16,900, somewhat low even at that time for a solid ceramic brick house with three bedrooms and two baths. The realtor explained that the house had been hard to sell because it was near the Jewish Country Club. That didn't bother Teena or me at all, but it does indicate the situation regarding race/ethnicity at that time in Nashville. (We visited the area a few years ago, and the house was still standing. Its appearance had been damaged because of an addition apparently designed to make it serviceable as a rental house, perhaps a duplex.)

DLC was definitely segregated racially. The only non-white people on campus were a few cooks and janitorial personnel. The president publicly discussed this, indicating his fear that some of our students might date the African-American personnel, whom he characterized as "lookers."

The Symphony was also segregated. A very fine African-American violinist auditioned for the Symphony and was told that he couldn't be admitted because of his color. This did not interfere with his inclusion in the recording studios, where he immediately was welcomed and where his contributions and leadership were appreciated. His name was Brenton Banks, and he and I became good friends. He taught at Tennessee A&I, where he had great musical equipment. At one time, I needed to borrow a bell chime for a concert at DLC, so I called Brenton. In a few minutes, a pickup truck arrived with bell chimes on it, and we used the chimes for a few weeks at no cost.

In recording sessions, when we had questions concerning the music we were playing, Brenton usually had the answers. He told us that we were recording music that originated in the black communities and was called "race" music. He had financed his education at Cleveland Institute of Music playing race music on piano in saloons on Saturday nights and again in church on Sundays (with different words). He often played blues on piano during sessions while the engineers checked "takes." He would start with a phrase or two and be joined by the drummer and the bass. Gradually, anyone else could join in, improvising for as long as time allowed.

Brenton was quite a hero in the black community. In addition to other gifts, he was a fine composer in the contemporary style. He was invited to contribute a composition to a festival of modern music sponsored by the Symphony (which performed the compositions in a special outdoor concert at the Parthenon). Having seen his name in the newspapers announcing the concert, many members of the black community attended, evidently expecting something like jazz. Brenton's composition was near the beginning of the program, and it was very austere in a style reminiscent of Schoenberg. The black members of the audience apparently were disappointed, and many of them left (not too quietly).

The level of cooperation among musicians in Nashville was rather striking. Members of the Symphony often played as "ringers" in the DLC Orchestra, which I conducted. I reciprocated in their orchestras as needed. Some of these fine musicians included Dr. Michael Semanitsky, Ovid Collins, Wilda Tinsley, Joan Mack, and Sam Hollingsworth. I can't remember more names, but there were many others.

Our daughter, Patricia Beth, was married to Greg Niemann many years after we left Nashville. I was to toast the bride and dance the first dance with her. I will try to recall my toast.

"Now is the time I have been dreading! The time to dance with the bride! I'm a fiddle-player, not a dancer. I have no rhythm from the waist down. But I'm sure we'll be all right, so everyone just ignore us for the next few minutes.

"Before we dance, I have to teach you a short music appreciation lesson. Please pay attention, because there *will* be a quiz later.

"The music I have chosen is from a recording on which I played the night Patty Beth was born. It's a Columbia Records LP featuring the singer George Morgan. The title of the record is *Golden Memories*, and it's mostly about little boys. There's 'Danny Boy,' 'Dear Little Boy of Mine,' and 'Mother Machree' (of course, that one could go either way), and then there's 'Mighty Like a Rose,' which has the refrain 'Don't know what to call him but he's mighty like a rose.'

"Like many Nashville recording sessions in those days, this one began at about 5:00 p.m. with the understanding that it would go on until we finished the album (twelve songs). I was concerned, because I believed our second child could be born at any time. My wife, Teena, had gone to Indiana for the birth because she particularly liked Dr. Buckingham and the Martinsville Hospital.

"I didn't know this at the time, but Teena's family tried to call the recording studio several times to tell me that our baby was definitely arriving. The studio receptionist accepted the calls but couldn't put them through to me because of company policy.

"It was a long, grueling session, like most sessions. We did retake after retake, trying to get the right 'feel.' We also wanted to eliminate all errors, since Columbia didn't generally splice tapes. Often we were so tired it was an effort just to put one more finger down on a string or draw one more bow.

"Eventually (at about 3:00 a.m.), we finished the session. I may have staggered a bit as we left the studio. On the way out, I met our secretary, who told me I was the father of a baby girl.

"Our dance music will be 'Mighty Like a Rose' from the record we cut the night Patty Beth was born."

Another recording session will perhaps complete an image of the recording scene in Nashville when we were there. (My days and nights seemed an endless treadmill of teaching, performing, and recording interrupted as necessary by meals, sleep, and family routines. Sometimes I was not sure whether it was day or night or exactly where I was located.) I was called to play an album with Ray Price (the Oklahoma Cowboy). The album was devoted completely to familiar old-time hymns except for one new song by Stuart Hamblen, composer of the popular "This Old House." The new song was called "You Must Have Faith," and the album was eventually called simply "Faith." The session began in early evening and was to continue until the album was completed. I had to be at school the next morning at eight for juries (final examinations of music students who had private lessons in performance for academic credit. The entire music faculty formed an audience for each solo performance, after which we offered written criticism and a suggested grade for the student. The grades would be averaged and combined with the teacher's grade. The combination would be reported as a semester grade.)

Ray Price's singing style is very touching to most audiences, and it was particularly effective when he recorded such hymns as "Softly and Tenderly Jesus is Calling." The orchestral and vocal backup arrangements were skillfully and tastefully done, and the performers had that adrenalin-fed feeling that something very special was taking place. Somewhat disconcerting was the occasional DAMN! That exploded from Ray Price when he made a mistake. "Softly and tenderly…DAMN! Let's do it again." This sounded especially inappropriate on playbacks, when the volume would be just shy of ear-splitting.

I don't know how he managed it, but at about 2:00 a.m., Mr. Price had a catered dinner served in the studio. On long tables with spotless white cloths there were roasted hams and turkeys, selections of bread, salads, and vegetables and (big mistake) cases of champagne and beer. Everyone was invited to partake, and the clock was allowed to run, meaning that we were paid recording scale while eating! I was wise enough to eat very little and drink only water, but not everyone was so wise. I don't know how we managed to complete the album, but we did, finishing at about 6:00 a.m. Owen Bradley, our A&R man, called Stuart Hamblen at his home and played "You Must Have Faith" for him on the telephone. Mr. Hamblen was so overcome by emotion that he could hardly speak. I received a copy of the LP later and played it for many visiting friends, almost always with similar results.

After the session, I arrived at home at about 6:30 a.m. and slept approximately one hour before going to school for juries. I felt groggy and rather nauseated.

The first jury was sung by a nubile young alto who performed the "Air" from Handel's *Israel in Egypt*. The text is: "Their land brought forth frogs, yea, even in the king's chambers. He gave their cattle over to the pestilence; blotches and blains broke forth on man and beast." As he often did in other compositions, Handel used much tone-painting in setting this text. So vivid is the setting that it affected me greatly in my somewhat weakened condition. I could almost see the frogs being squished between the feet of men and cattle covered in blotches and blains. Somehow I survived the juries without vomiting, but at times I was not confident of that outcome.

David Lipscomb College was extremely conservative when I taught there. In our official presentations, we often seemed to deny that the human body existed. We were somewhat like the medieval artists who painted or sculpted human beings as empty clothing with necks, wrists, and ankles attached. I was quite surprised when during juries (held in the library) I idly opened an art book, which had been left on the table we were using. Perhaps due to frequent usage, the book fell open to a Renaissance painting depicting several young ladies seated in a garden playing various instruments such as lyre, harp, flute, viol, and lute. It was a charming painting, unusual in that all the performers were nude! The entire music faculty was seated at the same table, including the department chairperson (Ms. Irma Lee Batey). I was one of the youngest members of the faculty, and I was conscious of their interest in my reaction to the painting. I was rather startled and surprised that the librarian had not painted clothing on the nude bodies before allowing the book to circulate. My stammered comment was "Wow! Chamber music at Lipscomb was never like that!" The entire music faculty broke out in laughter, beginning with the lowest rank and proceeding upward until Ms. Batey reluctantly joined in.

Two other aphorisms that were often repeated among the faculty may complete the depiction of the atmosphere at David Lipscomb College when I was there: "Lipscomb guarantees that your daughter will be a virgin when she graduates, even if she wasn't one when she came here" and "Sex is all right so long as you don't enjoy it."

22

After working in Nashville for four and one-half years, I knew that it was time to move on. The inspiration we had found at David Lipscomb College had eroded as we discovered the compromises that we had to make daily in order to survive. The slogan "Lipscomb is different" sounded hollow as we saw the same struggles there as elsewhere. I found a vacancy at Southeastern Louisiana College in Hammond, Louisiana, applied for it and was hired. We moved there in the summer of 1963, temporarily renting a small brick house and making plans to build a home.

Hammond, Louisiana, is about twenty-five miles east of Baton Rouge and thirty-five miles northwest of New Orleans, near Lake Ponchartrain. Baton Rouge is the home of Louisiana State University, where my predecessor Dr. Michael Galasso moved after teaching at SLC for about twelve years. I inherited the string program that Dr. Galasso developed, and I immediately recognized that he had done excellent work in a difficult situation. (He told me that he had started dozens of beginners on string instruments, only to have most of quit after a year or two. He learned to expect girls to stop playing strings when they began wearing lipstick and polishing their nails.) He was the concertmaster of the Baton Rouge Symphony at LSU: I became his assistant and concertmaster of the Summer Theatre Orchestra, which he conducted. Several of my students in Hammond were also members of the Baton Rouge Symphony: they rode in my car to rehearsals and performances.

Hammond was widely known as the strawberry capital of the world. I spent the first few days and nights with my family at the

Casa da Fresa (House of Strawberries) Hotel, a very old building that our children suspected was haunted.

The population of Hammond was a delightful mix of Sicilians (the strawberry farmers), Cajuns (originally *Arcadian*, from the group of French Canadians who settled in Nova Scotia in the eighteen century and were eventually driven out by the British), WASPs (White Anglo-Saxon Protestants), and African Americans. These ethnic groups were predominant, but there were probably others. While each group tried to maintain its ethnic identity, no racial tension was evident to me when we first moved there.

We built our house on reclaimed swamp land just a few minutes from the College. It was a very nice white brick modern rancher with four bedrooms, two baths, a kitchen, a dining room with adjoining living room, a breeze-way carport, and an attached area which contained a laundry and an office/practice room for me. Because it was on reclaimed swamp land, it was necessary to build the slab foundation and the footers in one piece (monolith) with heavy reinforcement bars spread throughout to avoid possible cracking as the house settled.

The creatures that lived in the swamp before it was filled in were loath to leave! We had families of armadillos living within a few feet of our house: almost every day at least one mother armadillo led her brood of babies down the street at a very slow speed. Drivers had two choices: wait for them or run over them. Most of us waited. We probably also had alligators, various turtles, and other swamp life, but we stayed clear of the areas where they might be.

The orchestra at SLC was actually a community orchestra that included the college-level string players and other instrumentalists as needed. It was called the Tangipahoa Parish Youth Orchestra (the state was organized in parishes, which were much like counties). The orchestra performed mostly string orchestra literature such as Handel and Corelli *Concerti Grossi*, Bach *Concertos* and *Suites*, and works by Mozart, Britten, Elgar, Vaughan Williams, and William Walton. Performances were generally at a high level. We were invited to play concerts over WDSU TV three times, which we did successfully. Several of our students eventually became professional musicians.

Two of them, Marjorie Sibley and John Wilcox, were selected by audition to perform the solo parts of Vivaldi's *Concerto in a minor for Two Violins* with the New Orleans Symphony.

The Tangipahoa Youth Orchestra toured frequently, especially during the fall months. We performed in public schools throughout the parish, hoping to encourage the orchestras in those schools. During that season, we had rain almost every day. Most of the parish was at sea level or below, and the water did not drain quickly. I couldn't count the number of times I pushed two timpani through several inches of water on the sidewalk to the bus.

To continue my Air Force Reserve duties I was assigned to New Orleans Naval Air Station where two reserve units were stationed, flying C119 cargo planes. I was never fully qualified to fly the C119, but I worked on it during my monthly weekend training periods. Shortly after, I was assigned there, one of the units was called to active duty in Vietnam. The unit was selected by drawing numbers out of a hat, and our unit was at risk to be drawn! I didn't find out about any of this until my next training period, which could easily have been in 'Nam.

My first experience with racism in Louisiana came during my first year at SLC. Dr. Galasso had a youth orchestra at LSU comparable with the one he had started at SLC. He called and suggested that we do a small tour of three schools in Baton Rouge with our two orchestras combined. I was delighted with the idea and immediately agreed to the suggestion.

I came home from training in New Orleans on a Sunday night shortly afterward. I was exhausted as usual after such a weekend, but I found a telephone call from the chairperson of the Music Department. I returned his call immediately. His first sentence was "I took the liberty of cancelling your plan to do concerts in Baton Rouge." I asked why, and he answered, "Didn't you know that one of the schools where you were planning to play is a black school?" I didn't know, and it wouldn't have mattered anyway. His last comment was "If you had done that concert you might have had a cross burned on your lawn." My fleeting thought was that I hoped they wouldn't damage our house! Perhaps we should designate a cross-burning area in our subdivision?

Another event that suggested strong racial feelings on campus: our dean of the College announced publicly that he would withdraw his daughter (who lived in the dormitory) from the college if one (African American) was placed there to live! That was in 1963!

We were happy in our new home, and I was generally happy at SLC, except for one problem: the swamp seemed to breed variants of flu and other short-term diseases to which I had not developed immunity. I was ill most of the time and had to prop myself against the piano in order to teach. I was glad that the season was changing to fall, hoping the germs would die for that year.

On November 22, I went home for lunch as usual (a convenience I appreciated very much). When I came back to school, it looked as though the whole music department was gathered in the lobby/auditorium entrance. They were dancing, singing, and generally celebrating. I asked what was going on, and a student answered, "Someone shot Kennedy, and it couldn't happen to a better guy!" I was forced to wonder what kind of place SLC was, and what was I doing there?

I was asked to take charge of the Summer Music Camp at SLC, one of the activities Dr. Galasso had directed. In a meeting with the Music faculty, I was asked to publicize the camp more than it had been publicized previously, which I was happy to do. I prepared news releases and publicity materials and released them widely. Our first camp was a success, with good attendance and much good instruction.

The second year of my camp direction was planned much like the first. A day for enrollment was announced. I was in my office early, waiting for our crop of campers. I heard a rather timid knock on my door. I opened it and there stood a small African American boy about eleven years old. He announced that he was there to enroll in camp. I instructed him to speak to the chairperson downstairs. In about five minutes, I received a call from the chairperson announcing that Summer Music Camp was cancelled for that year.

By the end of the first year, Teena and I decided that SLC was not the place for us! I resigned, but the dean didn't accept my resignation. In an interview with him, he told me that so many faculty members were leaving it would impossible to fill the vacant positions before the school year began. If I left at that time, he would give me a bad evaluation. If I remained for another year, he would evaluate me favorably and give me a good recommendation. I elected to stay another year.

Professor Ken Davis called from Harding College (Searcy, Arkansas) and asked if I would like to move there. I knew Ken from Indiana University where he studied for the doctorate degree while I was working on my master's degree in violin. I liked and respected him very much, but I recalled my experience with David Lipscomb College (a "sister" to Harding). I was also concerned that there were very limited performance opportunities for violinists at Harding. He proposed that the college donate one-half of my teaching hours to the Arkansas Symphony at Little Rock so that I could serve as concertmaster there. That seemed unique and appealing to me, so I accepted.

We sold our new house in Hammond, Louisiana, immediately and moved to Searcy where we could purchase faculty housing (another unusual benefit from Harding College).

23

Teena and I decided to leave Harding College (Searcy, Arkansas) in 1968, having moved there in 1965. I had enjoyed teaching there: the administration, faculty, and students were great, but we finally realized that we had outgrown the Church of Christ. (In addition, the Arkansas Symphony had collapsed after some scandal involving the conductor. Since my success at Harding depended greatly upon my position in the Symphony, there was added incentive to leave the school.)

A short time after we moved to Harding, I washed my car on a Sunday afternoon. I was denounced by a little neighbor girl (about seven years old) for profaning the Sabbath. Later, our eleven-year-old son was told that he was too old to swim in mixed groups (boys and girls). Husbands and wives were not allowed to swim together (wearing bathing suits) at summer camp because that had the appearance of evil. We had a self-appointed "inquisitor" who checked faculty members in private and public conversations to make sure that we believed correctly in matters such as millennialism (pre-, post-, and a-) and other rather arcane doctrines. Even though we thought of ourselves as conservative, we found it difficult to tolerate that atmosphere. One event finally reached the tipping point.

We had a very good string orchestra at Harding, with students from as far away as New York. We gave regular concerts in which we played standard works for string orchestra. We were not allowed to call our winter concert a Christmas concert, but it tended to coincide with the Christmas season because of typical institutional scheduling. Fortunately, most instrumental music can be listed on programs without mentioning religious connections (instrumental music was not allowed in worship). Our winter concert in 1967 included the famous *Christmas Concerto* by Corelli, which we listed simply as *Concerto*. The students prepared the concert carefully and played it beautifully.

Several days before the concert, some students suggested that we decorate the stage with sprigs of American holly, which grew in abundance nearby in the woods. I did not object, so the students gathered carloads of holly with a few leaves and several bright berries on each twig. They attached the sprigs to the proscenium with plastic tape, creating a beautiful Christmas card effect. The lovely stage contributed greatly to the effectiveness of the concert, which was much appreciated by the audience.

The following Sunday, our preacher devoted a considerable portion of his sermon to the condemnation of our concert, with special attention to the heathen decorations. For me and my wife this was the last straw. I announced my resignation the next day to our department chairman, agreeing to stay on for the rest of the year. We spent the summers of 1966 and 1967 at Indiana University (we still thought of Bloomington as our home). I was a graduate student doing work, which I hoped would lead to a doctoral degree (it was later accepted by transfer to Catholic University in Washington, DC). My violin teacher was Tadeusz Wronski from Poland.

Mr. Wronski spoke no English when he first arrived in the United States. I could speak *only* English, so we communicated by sign language and by illustration on the violin. However, he quickly "picked up" the English language since he spoke several other languages. He was a great violinist and teacher, one of his important achievements being the first violinist to perform the Alban Berg *Concerto*. He gave me a copy of this composition with his fingerings and bowings. He also gave me a copy of his edition of the Paganini *Caprices*. (It is almost as worn as my copy of the Brahms *Violin Concerto).*

Shortly after I met Mr. Wronski, I told him about my tour of duty in the USAF, including my experience as a pilot. He was fascinated with flying! I offered to take him for a ride in one of the Cessna 152 planes owned by the IU Flying Club (of which I was a member).

We scheduled the ride, and I took him to Kister's Field in my 1963 Pontiac, which he admired. (In Poland, owning a car like the Pontiac was for the select few, and flying privately in a small plane was practically unknown at that time.)

We arrived at the airport, I signed in and picked up the ignition key, and we boarded the Cessna after I demonstrated the preflight inspection. I checked the controls and found that I could not pull the yoke all the way back (necessary for full "up" elevator). I was somewhat alarmed until I discovered that Mr. Wronski's somewhat ample stomach was blocking free movement of the controls. We adjusted his seating, started the engine, and took off with me commenting on what I was doing.

As we left the runway, the little plane banked rather sharply to the right. I immediately corrected to straight and level flight, realizing that my passenger's ample stomach and rather stout physique was more than balancing my weight in the left seat!

As we reached cruising altitude, I invited Mr. Wronski to follow through on the controls, which he did with great enthusiasm. He would spot various familiar places on the ground and turn the plane so that he could see them more clearly. When we flew over the IU Music Building he exclaimed, "There's the Music Building!" and immediately dove toward it! I took control and returned to level flight, not wishing to interrupt anyone's rehearsal.

We returned to Kister's Field, parked the Cessna, and went for a short visit to Teena's parents' home.

One day, as I opened Mr. Wronski's door, he asked, "What is *pinkie?*" I couldn't think of an answer except that some people called pseudo-communists *pinkies.*

"No, no," said Mr. Wronski. "I have a student who can't seem to do anything I ask of her. She always says, 'It hurts my pinkie.'" I realized that she was complaining about her little finger! When I told Mr. Wronski that, he seemed relieved. He was concerned that it might be some embarrassing personal problem.

At that time, I usually had on my desk several notifications of vacancies in colleges and universities throughout the United States and several foreign countries. I chose Towson State College just north of Baltimore, Maryland, and applied there. I was accepted to begin teaching the following year (1968). Teena and I were excited to begin a new chapter in our lives. Our three children were too young to understand.

Although I had lived in Atlanta and our family had lived in Nashville, Baltimore was larger than any city we had called home. The colonial brick row houses of the inner city were mostly boarded up when we moved there. They were condemned and scheduled for restoration or demolition. The inner harbor was so polluted nothing could live there (according to local parlance, which usually continued "So the water must be safe to drink!"). There were many rats, and few lights. That part of the city had a ghostly appearance at night. Some other areas, such as Little Italy, were preserved much as they had been in colonial days. We soon learned the delights of visiting Little Italy and enjoying wonderful food at the small family restaurants there.

We were able to buy a solid ceramic Cape Cod colonial house with slate roof in north Baltimore (722 East Belvedere), just a few miles from Towson State College. Situated on a winding country lane surrounded with various styles of brick colonial homes, the lovely house was very attractive to us, and it was priced at $20,500! It was about thirty years old and in excellent condition. We didn't know that it was in a "changing neighborhood" (code words which meant that African-Americans were buying real estate there for the first time) and that a new parkway (Northern Parkway) was to be built just a few blocks north of Belvedere, causing all traffic to be shunted "temporarily" onto our narrow street! These were the reasons for the low price, which meant that resale of the house would be very difficult. (Years later, after moving from Baltimore, we returned for a visit and found that the parkway had been completed, the street had returned to its country lane appearance, the neighborhood had become integrated and stabilized, and that the house was worth more than $200,000.)

Teena and I loved Baltimore and especially the surrounding county. It had the appearance and atmosphere of colonial America, much like the eighteenth-century England we had seen in pictures and I had seen in my many visits there as an Air Force pilot.

Baltimore county was suburban, a place where wealthy people lived in colonial houses attached to immaculate horse farms with white board fences. They had organized fox-hunts complete with formally-dressed ladies and gentlemen, horn-players who blew signals to keep the hunt organized, even stirrup cups to sip before the hunts began. Colonial country inns dotted the landscape, still in business and situated very close to the roads as they had been in horse and buggy days. Wonderful meals were available with menu items very much like those of several hundred years before. It was some of the most beautiful real estate we had ever seen. Towson State College was situated on just such real estate, at that time unspoiled.

Towson State College began as a "normal" school, an appellation with somewhat ironic overtones. Such a school was a teacher-training institution which admitted only female students for the two-year curriculum required at that time for state certification as a public-school teacher. (In 1968, the school was a four-year college. It later became a university with a graduate division.) The buildings were well constructed of durable materials in a typical institutional style, which one could describe as neo-practical. The facilities were clearly designed for use by females, a minor inconvenience for males.

My assignment in the music department was to develop an orchestra, teach private violin and string classes, and teach one other course in music history or theory. The department had existed for only a few years, and few qualified music majors elected to attend there (most choosing either Peabody Conservatory or Goucher College). It was common for faculty members to recruit students by simply walking down the halls, engaging students in conversations, and suggesting that they might want to major in music because of the quality of their voices. I had not seen the Broadway musical *Music Man* at the time, but the method of recruitment employed in that musical was quite similar!

The orchestra consisted of two people, neither of whom was a student at the college. Phyllis Olson, a fine string bassist, was a part-time member of the faculty, and Thornton Packham was a retired accountant who played violin. I decided to follow the pattern of development used by Dean Bain when he arrived at Indiana

University where the orchestra program was already somewhat more mature.

(Dean Bain believed that musical education consisted of studying and performing great music under conditions that allowed for a good representation of appropriate musical style. He accomplished this by assembling students in positions where they could function well, augmenting the resulting ensemble with sufficient numbers of professional-level players to ensure successful performances. He hired the Berkshire String Quartet in residence and formed a professional woodwind quintet from faculty members already in residence. He also hired at least one faculty member to teach each orchestral instrument. All of those faculty members participated regularly in IU Philharmonic rehearsals and concerts, serving as assistant section leaders and giving on-the-job training to student members. Advanced students served as section leaders and occasional soloists in standard concertos.)

At TSC, I applied for and received a grant from the Trust Funds of the Musicians Union so that I could hire a nucleus of musicians from the Baltimore Symphony and add college students, faculty, and amateurs from the community to form an orchestra. I treated the Baltimore Symphony as a community cultural resource, encouraging our students to attend professional concerts and to play alongside professional musicians in rehearsals and concerts at the school. My purpose was not to produce professional performers: I wanted to produce musically educated teachers who could assist their students in making intelligent choices of the music that influenced their lives. Most of our students were from the first generations of their families to attend college. They were also mostly from poor families with very limited cultural backgrounds.

The TSC Orchestra gave its first performance in the barely adequate auditorium of the Demonstration School on campus as a part of a departmental concert. The group of about fifteen string players performed *London Street Cries* by Orlando Gibbons. After the performance, one of the professional players from the BSO whom I had known at Indiana University made a comment, which I took as a compliment: "It's always better to play good music badly than to play bad music badly."

24

Soon after I arrived at TSC Dale Rauschenberg, the percussion teacher whom I had known when we were students at Indiana University recommended me to play in the orchestra at Morris A. Mechanic Theater in Baltimore. I was surprised but grateful for the opportunity.

I arrived at the appointed rehearsal time to play in my first show, *I Do! I Do!*, starring Robert Preston and Mary Martin. The typical pit orchestra of about twenty players began rehearsal with me in the violin section. After about thirty minutes, we came to a song called *Where Are the Snows of Yesteryear?* which began with a violin solo. The conductor asked several violinists to play the solo, including me. I was chosen to be the performer and also the concertmaster of the orchestra, the position that I continued to occupy for the ten years I was in Baltimore. I was also invited to play as concertmaster of the Painter's Mill Music Fair and the Merriwether Post Pavilion orchestras as well as many orchestras for single engagements such as church services and seasonal choral performances. Sometimes all three theaters would schedule shows, which required string sections, and I would be asked to choose a show to play while serving as subcontractor for strings in the other two theaters. This completely unexpected development led to many enjoyable friendships and experiences, including appearances with Bob Hope, Frank Sinatra, Jack Benny, Henry Mancini, Liberace, Rock Hudson, Eddy Arnold, Perry Como and many others. I was also able to recommend many of my students for engagements as they advanced to the necessary performance level. I still remember *Where Are the Snows of Yesteryear?* in A-flat major.

My usual stand-partner at Morris A. Mechanic Theatre was Isadore (Izzy) Bransky, a seventy-eight-year-old violinist who studied as a child with the famous violinist/teacher Hans Sitt in Leipzig, Germany. Izzy told me many stories about his student days as well as his days as a professional violinist. He also told me that his vision was poor and that he would not be able to read music well, but he could hear me and imitate my playing the second time through the music. I had doubts about that but discovered it to be true. I could see that Izzy's hands had been deformed by arthritis, but when he placed his violin under his chin, he looked and sounded like a violinist. I respected contractor Feen Iula for many reasons, one of which was his employment of musicians such as Izzy, who had a lifetime of great experience but little or no provision for retirement.

I have been fortunate to experience many links to the history of music. Izzy was one of these: he studied the Mendelssohn *Concerto in e minor* with Hans Sitt when it was still in manuscript! On one occasion, Sitt had to go on tour for a few weeks, so he assigned the Mendelssohn to twelve-year-old Izzy with instructions to edit the manuscript (fingerings and bowings) and learn to play it while Sitt was absent. Izzy did his best with this formidable assignment, but Sitt was not pleased. He expressed his great displeasure in rather graphic terms! I was fascinated to know that my stand-partner knew the Mendelssohn *Concerto* when it was "contemporary" music!

When Izzy arrived in America to begin his career his first employment was at the Roxy Theatre on Broadway in New York. Many European musicians, especially Jewish ones, began in that way in the United States, using their Hebrew names until they became established, after which they often adopted more American-sounding names. Some of them attained great fame: Izzy knew them when they played with him in the Roxy Theatre. I met one of them at the Morris A. Mechanic Theater.

The musical *Fiddler on the Roof* visited Baltimore at least three times while I played at the Mechanic Theater. The show ran two or three weeks each time (seven performances each week). It was based in New York, and the touring group was excellent. Although they had performed the show hundreds of times in many different situations, they strived to make each performance better than the previous one. (For the first engagement in Baltimore, they brought their own concertmaster, and I served as his assistant.)

At the first rehearsal, I met the visiting concertmaster, but I didn't recognize his name. He was older than me by quite a few years. As the rest of the violinists arrived, they became quite excited: Joseph Stopak was the concertmaster! They explained to me that he was a famous concert violinist in the thirties, touring as soloist, playing as featured artist on network radio, and serving as concertmaster of the Roxy Theater Orchestra in New York. I was greatly honored to meet him and to play alongside him for several weeks.

Mr. Stopak and I had dinner together several times during the engagement, and we talked about many things, including *Fiddler on the Roof.* He had toured worldwide with the show, and he discovered that people of greatly differing cultures thought the story was about *their* culture. This was especially surprising when they played in China! *Fiddler* is a very Jewish show in every respect, and Mr. Stopak could recall incidents from his boyhood that were very much like incidents in the show.

When *Fiddler* returned for subsequent engagements in Baltimore, I was concertmaster. I remembered the way Mr. Stopak played the solos, and I tried to imitate him. I must have succeeded to some degree: I actually had compliments to the effect that I "played good, not to be Jewish"!

Many amateur theater organizations produced *Fiddler*, not realizing how difficult it was until they had already committed themselves. One such group called me to play the solos and be concertmaster of their production, which I was happy to do. I was to do two rehearsals and three performances. This arrangement was changed before I began rehearsals.

I received a telephone call in which I was told that after rehearsal the previous evening the conductor (whom I had never met) went out to his car, sat down, and *died!* The caller asked whether I would consent to conduct the production. Under the circumstances I could hardly refuse, especially since I had played the show about thirty times. I immediately called Collette Wichert, a graduate student at

Towson State and an excellent violinist, asking her to replace me as concertmaster. She was willing to do this, for which I was very grateful. After two rehearsals, we performed the show quite successfully, although I had to adjust from a cast of (world famous) thorough professionals to a cast of local amateurs with various amounts of training and experience.

25

Having served in the Air Force as a pilot, I was required to spend an additional seven years as an active reserve pilot. In Arkansas, there had been no reserve unit within practical travelling range, so I was allowed to resign my Air Force commission and be commissioned in the Army National Guard to fly O1A observation planes (also known as the *Bird Dog*). When I arrived in Baltimore, I tried to revert back to the Air Force but found that was against current policy. The nearest National Guard base I could find was at Edgewood Arsenal, approximately twenty miles from my home through some very heavy traffic. I was assigned there and tried to make the situation work, but without much success. The war was raging in Vietnam, and all but two O1A planes were over there. Many times I would drive all the way to Edgewood Arsenal only to find that the two planes I was qualified to fly were either out of commission or already taken by someone else. I struggled with the situation for about two years, after which I was told that my reserve obligation had been met, and I would be discharged from the National Guard.

(I had been in the National Guard unit at Little Rock when the Rev. Martin Luther King was assassinated in Memphis, sixty miles away. Due to the ensuing riots in Little Rock, our National Guard unit was activated, including me. Since no flying was needed in the situation, I was assigned to haul troops to and from the armory to the state capitol building to man four fifty-caliber machine guns set up in the main corridors of the capitol. They were aimed at the large entry doors, and the troops had orders to fire if anyone forced entry into the capitol. Fortunately, we had a cold rain and the feared large riot did not materialize.)

When we arrived in Baltimore a few weeks later, we found whole city blocks that had been burned during riots associated with the racial unrest that had culminated in the King assassination. My new National Guard unit was activated to control the riots, including me (again). Since I was new to the unit, I was assigned to read training manuals related to my duties for the two weeks of our activation.

Most of the ten-year period we spent at TSC was a time of great unrest. The war in Vietnam, the scandal associated with Water Gate, and the incredible political corruption in Baltimore and Baltimore County all added to the normal complexity of starting an orchestra at TSC and becoming established as a member of the academic community there. Former County Executive Spiro T. Agnew, who became governor of Maryland and later vice president of the United States under President Richard Nixon, was the father of one of our students at TSC. He was also inevitably a major influence on the campus because of his former positions as county executive and governor. His attitudes toward the Vietnam War and toward the many protestors were often stated in picturesque terms not designed to foster understanding and cooperation. His skill with words was put to a test later when he pleaded *nolo contendere* to charges that required him to resign as vice-president. He convinced many of his followers that it meant "not guilty"! Later he was invited to appear on the Bob Hope Show at Painter's Mill Music Fair (where I played in the pit orchestra), and the capacity audience gave Mr. Agnew a resounding standing ovation!

Our students and faculty reacted to the whole situation with shrill and unrestrained (not to mention frequently crude) speech and behavior. Many people treated the college as a vehicle to avoid military service and to object violently to the war and to the government generally. The college administration adopted policies that allowed people to enroll as students, avoid being drafted into the military, avoid class attendance and participation, and to have failing grades expunged from their records so that there was no evidence that they had ever registered for courses. They could repeat the process indefinitely and circumvent the purposes of draft deferment. I heard rumors that some of our music majors were admitted to our department as a result of phone calls from state senators, bypassing entrance exams and other admission requirements. This led to the presence of music majors who could not read the most basic musical notation, which meant that we had to offer remedial courses in an effort to bring such students up to entry level.

Frequently, students would skip classes in order to participate in demonstrations at prominent buildings in nearby Washington, DC. Some of my students announced to me that they would not be in class, told me the time and place of a demonstration, and *assigned* me to be at the demonstration in lieu of teaching! I quickly learned the meaning of the word *chutzpah*, new to me at the time! I also remember one interview of a prospective string bass major: our faculty committee asked him the usual questions about his experience and plans for education at TSC. After the preliminaries, we asked him what he planned to play for his entrance audition. He answered that he didn't plan to play. In fact, he didn't own a bass. He wanted to take all the lessons and practice later when he could afford an instrument!

Eileen Marconi, one of my violin students, asked me to give her a ride to nearby Fort McHenry. She had heard that there was a part-time vacancy for a person to sell chewing gum in the souvenir shop. She applied for the job and was told that she had to take a civil-service examination since Fort McHenry was a federal institution. She duly completed the exam with high grades and was offered a full-time position with the Air Force as a buyer for jet fighter planes! She accepted the offer, which was a great opportunity for her, but I had mixed feelings about it: she was one of my best violin majors!

Several students assigned to my classes attended class only once (the first day). I would not see them again until final examination, when they would come to class and tell me that if they didn't receive an "A" in my course, they would be drafted into the army and sent to Vietnam. Ironically, I was in Special Reserve Forces subject to assignment in Vietnam with only twenty-four-hour notice. Somehow, I didn't feel great sympathy for those students.

O1A pilots in Vietnam usually served as "spotters" for jet fighter bombers that were circling high overhead waiting for a signal to attack. A spotter pilot would fly far below at treetop height over the jungle, searching for the very elusive enemy, being careful to fly straight and level at slow speed while the observer in the back seat studied the location, size, and layout of the enemy force on the ground. When a suitable target was located, the O1A pilot would fire a smoke rocket into the center of the target, open the throttle of his plane, and turn suddenly away from the approaching jet during the one or two minutes necessary for it to arrive at the scene and obliterate it. Since the enemy soon discovered the purpose of "bird-dog" aircraft, spotter duty became extremely dangerous because of small-arms fire from the ground. Average life expectancy for bird-dog pilots was estimated in days, according to rumors that I had heard.

(I barely missed being assigned to Vietnam twice before we moved to Baltimore. The first time was when we were in the New Orleans area and I was assigned to a C-119 outfit. There were two such groups at the naval air station, and one was to be sent to Vietnam, selected by drawing numbers from a hat. Our sister group was selected, all this happening while I was absent from the base. I was informed at the next scheduled training period.

(When Teena and I decided to move from Louisiana to Harding College in Arkansas, my next military assignment was to be at Memphis [TN] Naval Air Station flying C-123 aircraft. I was asked whether I wanted to carry my medical records or have the Air Force send them. Since I wanted to take a two-week leave of absence, I opted to carry the records. Technically, this meant that I was unassigned until my planned reporting for duty at Memphis.

(We arrived in Arkansas, and I called Memphis to report my availability for duty. A master sergeant answered the phone. "You're just a little bit late. Our entire unit was shipped out for Vietnam last week. There's nothing here but me and a filing cabinet." Since there was no Air Force Reserve unit nearby, I resigned my Air Force commission and accepted an Army commission so that I could join the National Guard and fly O1A planes as a member of Special Reserve Forces. This unit was on twenty-four-hour notice to report to Vietnam.)

26

Teena and I had decided before moving to Baltimore that we would change our church affiliation. We found Grace United Methodist Church on Charles Street, a short distance from our home on East Belvedere. Attracted to the building, we decided to visit there. It was the best decision we could have made. We had stumbled upon one of the very most highly regarded churches in the entire region. We didn't feel a need to "shop" further.

Grace Church, as we called it, was a medium-sized congregation with an excellent minister (Dr. Norman van Brunt), who was assigned there shortly after we arrived, and an excellent organist/director of music (Bruce Eicher, who is still in the same position more than forty years later). Mrs. (Martha) van Brunt must be mentioned as part of the ministry since she was very active in the program of the church. There was a quartet of professional soloists, one of whom was the bass James Morris, a student at Peabody Conservatory at the time who later became the leading bass of the Metropolitan Opera. I was soon invited to participate as violinist when needed, and we often performed music for choir, soloists, organ and strings or small full orchestra. The word *performed* is appropriate as an indicator of the quality of preparation, but it is inadequate as a descriptor of the attitude of worship when we played/sang. Apparently, everything the congregation did was with an attitude of complete devotion, whether it was teaching a class, singing a solo, or preparing food for one of our frequent congregational meals. The entire program of the church was viewed as a work of art, with balance, taste, progression, sophistication, simplicity, and sense of direction. (We felt that our church experience was a sampling of heaven.) Whenever possible, I incorporated students and faculty from Towson State College into the music of Grace Church because I felt that this offered them opportunities for experience unmatched in the community.

As our orchestra at TSC continued to develop, we established a pattern of three concerts per year. Our fall concert was just before Christmas vacation, our spring concert near Easter, and a concerto concert early in the spring semester. We later added a summer concert since the Baltimore Symphony had no summer program at the time. The other colleges in the area also had no summer orchestra program so far as I could determine. On our regular concerts, we typically played an overture, a major work for string orchestra, and a symphony. The most difficult work we performed was *Rounds for String Orchestra* by David Diamond. Actually, this was too difficult, as I well knew, but I allowed my students to persuade me to program it. They learned a lot from the experience, but I dread to remember how the audience must have felt about it!

On the concerto concert, we usually programmed an overture, one movement of a major piano concerto, at least one movement or short work for another instrumental soloist, and at least one opera aria. On one such concert, we programmed one of my favorite vocal compositions, *Knoxville, Summer of 1915* by Samuel Barber with an undergraduate soprano whose name I can't remember. I was especially proud that we could offer this experience to her as well as to members of the orchestra and to the audience. For most of our students, such an opportunity was rare or nonexistent.

I was interested in completing my doctorate in violin, having studied two summers at Indiana University after completing my MM in violin there. I would have to be in residence at IU for at least three years in order to complete a doctorate, impossible at that time because of my other responsibilities. I discovered that Catholic University in Washington would allow half-time residence credit for doctoral candidates who carried at least six hours of courses (twelve being the minimum for full-time candidates). This seemed attractive and workable for me. I also discovered that CU had a list of approved violin teachers in Washington, New York, Baltimore, and Philadelphia, another great advantage for me.

I attended a violin recital in Baltimore a few years after arriving at Towson State College. It was a rather unusual recital with some new compositions heavily laden with symbolism. One movement I recall was played completely on the "e" string, tuned down an octave! It was a sort of frustrated love song made flabby by the very limp "e" string augmented by a slow and wide vibrato. After the recital, I heard someone ask a distinguished-looking gentleman if he had ever played that selection. His reply: "No, and I will go to my grave having never played it." A few minutes later, I was introduced to him. He was violinist Berl Senofsky, a winner of the prestigious Queen Elizabeth of Belgium Contest and faculty member of Peabody Conservatory in Baltimore! I asked about studying with him in the doctoral program at CU, and he said that he thought it might be arranged. Thus began my quest for the doctor of musical arts degree in violin.

The doctor of music in violin (DMA) at Catholic University is a performance degree comparable to the doctor of philosophy (PhD) except that emphasis is upon performance rather than research. Prospective candidates are required to prepare a recital that demonstrates their capacity to complete the degree. A faculty committee chooses to hear any part of the recital or the complete program. My committee asked for movements of unaccompanied Bach and a portion of the other works offered. I was accepted to begin course work as required for the degree. Mr. Senofsky was approved as my teacher. I could study with him at Peabody Conservatory in Baltimore.

A minimum of sixty hours of graduate course work is required for the DMA. My concentrations were music theory and music history with a few other courses. I travelled to CU for each course, often on Saturday mornings. Since much of the work required memorization, I recorded the texts on my portable tape recorder and played them as I drove back and forth to Washington, DC.

After completion of course work, I was examined and advanced to candidacy for the degree. The period of candidacy was a time for required recitals, a lecture-recital, a chamber music recital, a concerto recital, a typical college faculty recital, and a graduation recital. Recitals were open to the public, and the faculty committee was always there to evaluate. If a recital failed to pass, the candidate could prepare and perform again. Each performance cost six hundred dollars in fees, which served as incentive to make sure it passed! Performance literature was assigned by the committee chairperson in consultation with the candidate. The chairperson also assigned the date and time of each recital.

The concerto recital was most difficult. Three concertos were required, one of which could be either Baroque or Classical, and one each were to represent the Romantic and the Contemporary periods. The entire recital was to be forty-five minutes in length! This eliminated most of the Romantic and some of the Contemporary concerti. I chose the Bach *a minor*, the Bruch *g minor*, and the Samuel Barber. I was not at all sure that I could pass this hurdle, and I was greatly relieved when the committee announced that I had passed!

I had begun work toward the DMA with no illusions! I knew of very capable violinists who were not able to complete the degree. Many of my friends tried to discourage me, saying that I would be doing the same thing with a doctorate that I was doing without it. Yet every task was inspiring to me, and I could use in my daily work what I had learned. I felt myself being stretched almost to the breaking point. I did not think of completion of the degree: I was satisfied if I could complete the next task! Yet somehow, after seven years of hard work, I arrived at the last requirement: the graduation recital!

I didn't allow myself to consider that this was the *last* recital. I simply concentrated upon playing as well as I could. As I arrived at the last page of the Stravinsky *Duo*, I thought, "In about five minutes, I *could* be addressed as Dr. Richardson!" I was.

Besides the satisfaction endemic to the completion of the degree, I found that I was more employable with it. In addition, my salary reflected the new degree. I tried to compute how much more my earnings with the doctorate were compared to what they would have been without it. This is difficult to compare, but I concluded that my total earnings with the doctorate were about *half a million dollars* more than they would have been without it. This is *not* the reason to complete a doctorate, but it is a good return on the investment.

27

As professor of violin and conductor of the TSC community orchestra, I was frequently invited to perform violin recitals and chamber music concerts in the Baltimore/Washington areas. I also was invited to conduct symphony orchestras as guest conductor.

The Annapolis Symphony, many of whose members were also members of the Naval Academy Band, invited me to guest-conduct a concert during my second year at TSC. Their regular conductor had been diagnosed with cancer and was under intensive treatment, which prevented his conducting their spring concert two weeks later. He had prepared the concert, and I was asked to rehearse several times and conduct the performance. The program: *Fanfare for the Common Man* (Aaron Copland), *The Flower Clock* (Jean Francaix), and *Symphony No. 2 in D minor* (Cesar Franck). I hesitated to accept the engagement, but my students at TSC strongly encouraged me. I accepted and enjoyed the experience very much. Later, I was asked if I would become permanent conductor of the Annapolis Symphony! I didn't see how I could undertake that because of my already heavy schedule, so I reluctantly declined. I was very much surprised later to hear that Leon Fleisher, the famous pianist and member of the Peabody Conservatory Faculty, had accepted the appointment! He continued there for a number of years and succeeded admirably.

Perhaps the most memorable concert during my tenure at TSC began as a demonstration of the refurbished organ at Grace Memorial United Methodist Church. Teena and I had become members of that church, and I had become established as a violinist there. The organist/music director Bruce Eicher asked whether the

TSC Community Orchestra could cooperate in a joint concert to introduce the organ to the Baltimore community. I thought it was a good idea, so we planned a concert to include the Poulenc *Organ Concerto*, the Haydn *Little Organ Mass* with choir and soloists, and the Saint-Saens *Symphony No. 3 (Organ Symphony)*. Bruce Eicher was to be organ soloist in the Poulenc and to play organ in the other two selections.

A number of circumstances combined to make this rather routine plan a truly memorable occasion (Sunday, March 5, 1972). The Baltimore Symphony had been on strike for several weeks, and the community was starving for symphonic music. Also, the musicians whom I usually employed for our concerts were available and had extra time to prepare their parts. The church had spent $200,000 for refurbishment and expansion of the organ, and the community was excited to have an opportunity to hear the results. It was a gorgeous spring day with warm sunshine and millions of flowers in bloom on North Charles Street.

Dress Rehearsal on Saturday afternoon, March 4, had been miserable. There were childish mistakes of many kinds, leading me to believe that we had bitten off more than we could chew. Near the end of the rehearsal, I remarked that if the players didn't go home and practice their parts this event was headed for disaster! Next day, I believed they had paid attention.

Two hours before our concert time (4:00 p.m.), I was surprised to see that there was a terrific traffic jam covering the area within a mile of the church. The parking lot was soon filled, and cars were being parked in every conceivable spot within walking distance. I didn't know what was happening, but I was worried that there wouldn't be enough space left for our audience to park. Then the thought came: *Could this be our audience?* It was!

Well, before time for the concert to begin all seats were full, all folding chairs were out, people were sitting in all available places in the chancel, all windows were open, and people were sitting/standing outside to hear the concert, all doors were open, and people were standing in the hallways. Happily, no fire marshals seemed to be in attendance.

There was one small error: my name had been left off the program! Every organ pipe was described and its size shown, all instrumentalists and vocalists were named, and every other detail usually found on programs was there. Dr. Norman van Brunt, our pastor, spoke to correct the situation. He apologized for the mistake and then gave my name and described me as if I were an organ pipe!

From the first note of the Poulenc, I was encouraged to believe that the orchestra members had studied their parts. Everything seemed to be in place, and the performance was better than I had ever hoped it could be. The Saint-Saens Symphony brought the concert to a climax that had the audience on its feet yelling and applauding for about ten minutes. An offering was accepted, and I saw three or four large baskets heaped with money. I don't know how much was collected, but I heard that it was in the thousands of dollars.

I was delighted to know that a recording of the concert had been made. Well, sort of! The Poulenc and the Haydn were well-recorded, but the operator thought he would run out of tape before the end of the Saint-Saens. He changed the speed from seven and a half to three and three-fourths inches per second, which reduced the fidelity drastically. Later in the concert, the power supply burned out, first one then both channels, just at the climax of the last movement. I made the decision that I would purchase a good tape machine and be responsible for recording from that time on, which I did!

28

I had been teaching at Towson State University (the name had been changed without much additional change) for about nine years when I decided that I wanted a new position. My work was successful and the need for it seemed great. I was tenured and could have remained at TSU until retirement, but I was tired of the same old hopeless conflicts that began a few years after I arrived at Towson and seemed to grow as the school expanded.

One source of conflict was the utilization of real estate: architectural monstrosities built by TSU covered much of the beautiful Baltimore County scenery that had attracted me and my family. The school finally completed the new Fine Arts Building, a travesty of design and function from the beginning of its incorporation into campus life. The auditorium had poor acoustics, probably a result of its all-brick parallel-wall construction. A new pipe-organ had been installed in a room whose roof leaked and filled the pipes with water. Two large fans had been installed to circulate air from the heating/cooling system, but the fans worked in opposition so that the air would cycle between compression and expansion in a manner that created continuous vibrations at the lowest audible frequencies *(in a fine arts auditorium!)*. There were numerous settlement cracks in the concrete-block walls, one such crack preventing my office door from being locked. I could not leave my violin or other personal property there.

Each of the three departments in the Division of Fine Arts had been asked to design its section of the new building. This resulted in different ceiling heights of the three sections of the building, a problem solved by concrete ramp connections between the different heights. Another result of this independent planning was that the "life-drawing room" (nude painting) had a huge window that faced the rest of the building, which had ample numbers of windows allowing excellent (although somewhat distracting) observation of life-drawing to students in classrooms and professors in their offices.

Not surprisingly, the attractions of beautiful real estate so close to Baltimore tempted administrators and others to use college-owned facilities for commercial purposes. Our new gym and related facilities were rented to the Baltimore Colts for practice with the result that students and faculty members from the school had to limit their uses of those facilities. The same attitude seemed to inspire the announcement that sponsors of student performances could not schedule the new Fine Arts Auditorium for events unlikely to attract large audiences.

Our difficulties expanded far beyond real estate and building design. The Music Department seemed divided into two factions in open warfare which raged in faculty and committee meetings as well as concerts and other public activities of the department. There were accusations of racism in hiring, promoting, and tenure-granting procedures. This led to a pending lawsuit at the time when I left: I never heard the outcome of this, but since I was a member of the Tenure Committee, I was acquainted with some of the preliminary maneuvering.

Some students and faculty members participated in attempts to sabotage concerts. One of my planned orchestral concerts was cancelled because of sabotage. Another was seriously damaged. That a considerable amount of good work continued in our department is testimony to the maturity and professional capability of quite a few students and faculty members.

I applied for and received an unpaid leave of absence for one year in order to accept a position as associate professor at Lebanon Valley College in Annville, Pennsylvania. The leave of absence (rather than outright resignation) was to serve as a sort of spare tire to be used in case the position at LVC didn't turn out well.

Such caution seemed unnecessary when we arrived at LVC in the fall of 1978. The small liberal arts college, affiliated with the United Methodist Church, enjoyed a favorable reputation locally and nationally. The lovely campus was dominated by an excellent music building and an impressive chapel. (The cost of construction of the music building had been paid in full when the building was completed.)

Enrollment at the college was at optimal level for the size of the campus. The campus church was populated mainly by college administration, faculty, staff, and students; and the worship music was of very high quality comparable with that of much larger congregations in major cities. I was able to live in faculty guest housing four nights per week while arranging to build a house in Mt. Gretna, a lovely residential community. My family was to remain in Randallstown, Maryland, for the first year as they finished school commitments.

I was appointed by the dean as associate professor in the music department with the promise of tenure after one year. This corresponded with my plan to resign at Towson State at the completion of a one-year leave of absence. I was also appointed concertmaster/assistant conductor of the York (PA) Symphony with Dr. James Christian Pfohl, conductor. (Dr. Pfohl was the founder and for twenty-six years director of Brevard Music Center in North Carolina.) I was satisfied with my new position, and I made plans to stay there permanently, resigning my position at Towson State. These plans were to be altered considerably and quickly!

During the summer after my spring-time appointment at LVC, the Music Department chairperson was replaced. This did not trouble me since another member of the department became the replacement, and the former chairperson remained as a member of the faculty. However, this seems in retrospect to be the first movement down a slippery slope, which ended in chaos at the college.

The first year progressed rather normally except that the dean of the college was forced out of his position after serving many years. Being new on the faculty, I was scarcely aware of the underlying politics, but I heard vicious rumors. The change affected me primarily in that my promise of tenure had been made verbally by the dean

174

who was replaced. (Somehow the fulfillment of this promise never occurred!) My classes progressed rather normally, and the orchestra developed and performed well as expected. A new faculty member, organist Dr. Timothy Albrecht invited me to play with him several times at his church, which I did with great pleasure. Later, he played several organ concertos with the orchestra that I conducted. We had several fine organs on campus, and it was convenient to combine orchestra with that instrument and chorus. The design of the chapel presented a problem: the organ was at the back, which necessitated that members of the audience turn around in their seats if they wished to see the performers. (I can testify that this resulted in sore necks.)

We had regular chapel once each week (attendance not required). Dr. Albrecht conducted the choir and played organ. The music was excellent in every respect, but almost no one attended except the chaplain and a few students and faculty. Often the small choir out-numbered the congregation.

During the first year, I was invited to the Belgian Consulate in New York to receive a medal from the Ysaye Foundation (named for the famous violinist/composer Eugen Ysaye). The medal was presented in recognition of my playing the Ysaye *Sonata, Opus 27, No. 2* in Baltimore and Washington, DC, before leaving Towson State. I was quite surprised to be so honored, but I greatly appreciated the recognition. I was received by the consul along with about twenty other guests from many parts of the world. We enjoyed some champagne and hors d'oeuvres before the presentation of medals. *(No beechnuts or cold spring water were served.)* Later my name was added to the letterhead of the Ysaye Foundation along with the names of some very famous violinists. I felt that I didn't deserve the distinction, but I certainly enjoyed it!

The first year at LVC was disturbed by rumors that our college president was under attack and might be replaced. Newspaper stories gave some details, but generally, I was out of the loop and didn't hear much. Eventually, the newspaper carried a story saying that he was to remain as president because he had arranged to finance a new science building on the campus. Soon after that, story our new dean called a meeting of the music department in which he announced that some faculty positions would be lost unless we increased our enrollment to cover the cost of *"servicing"* the mortgage on our building. A number of faculty members were outraged, reminding the dean that they had worked to raise the money to pay for the music building and that it was paid in full at completion. The dean then announced that the president had mortgaged our building in order to build the new science building! We completed the year in an atmosphere of unrest and insecurity.

We spent the summer of 1979 finishing our move from Randallstown (MD) to Mt. Gretna. Our house was incomplete, but we were able to move in with bare studs where some walls were to be. All the essentials of plumbing, heating, and water well were installed and functioning. I did much of the work myself, acting as contractor for the rest. There were difficulties with our well, the water supply being barely adequate, so we drilled another well, which was totally dry. Less than fifty feet away, our neighbor had a well that produced more water than he could pump! Temporarily, we borrowed some of his water by attaching a hose to one of his faucets and connecting it to one of ours. Even though we had some setbacks, we loved Mt. Gretna and we were happy that we had moved there. I started a private violin studio in the lower floor, and our eldest son, Ernest, taught with me. We had excellent, talented students, some of whom are now enjoying careers as professional violinists.

We began the new school year (1979) in an atmosphere of uncertainty. Enrollment was down substantially, reaching a level below optimal for operation of the college. There was discussion about minimum enrollment required for the college to remain in operation. The usual sources of funds for the college were no longer reliable, resulting in very low funding. The national economy was in serious trouble under the Carter Administration. (We had finished our house and applied for a permanent mortgage, which we received at a much higher rate of interest than we had planned.) One member of our music faculty often expressed his concern for the situation in concrete terms: "We have to get those dormitory beds filled!" I had never before heard student enrollment described in those terms, but perhaps that standard of measurement was adequate.

Rumor had it that several co-eds were trying to "fill those beds," at least in the men's dormitory. A few of my students were said to spend their nights in that heroic undertaking. They were the same students who most needed to be studying and practicing in their chosen field: music.

I was requested to serve as a member of the Faculty Disciplinary Committee, which reviewed cases of egregious violations of rules by students. A few of the more colorful breaches of discipline may illustrate the behavioral atmosphere that was tolerated at LVC at that time and that tended to add to the difficulty of recruitment of violin majors.

Two students were carrying on a sort of feud for several days. One night, one of the students poured lighter fluid on the floor outside the door of the dormitory room where the other was sleeping, allowing the fluid to flow under the door and into the room. He then set the fluid on fire outside the door, allowing the flame to go under it. A pile of magazines was ignited, filling the room with smoke and risking a general conflagration. Fortunately, the sleeping student awakened and extinguished the flame before great harm was done. The members of the Committee observed that this was attempted arson under conditions which easily could have resulted in death. The guilty student argued that his offense was just a prank that was often done by other students in the dormitory.

In another case (also involving fire), a group a students placed an old reclining chair on the railroad tracks that ran through the campus. They then saturated the chair with some kind of inflammable fluid and waited for the scheduled train to arrive. As the train approached, they ignited the chair. The train hit the burning chair and dragged it several hundred feet past dry weeds and brush before it could stop. Fortunately, there were no injuries, and damage to property was minimal. The Committee decided after discussion that we had jurisdiction in the case, rather than local law enforcement officers. We decided that an appropriate penalty was to disqualify the guilty students from participation in competitive sports for one *summer*. (There were no competitive sports during summer.)

At that time in Pennsylvania, it was illegal to serve alcoholic beverages to students on campus. LVC rules of behavior also forbade alcoholic beverages and drugs. Nevertheless, every Friday afternoon, a beer truck would arrive on campus, park between the two dormitories, and unload kegs of beer for the weekend. There were widespread rumors that using drugs and drinking alcoholic beverages were rampant on campus. No case involving such behavior was referred to the Committee while I was a member.

We owned two cars at that time: an Oldsmobile Delta 88 and a Honda Civic. We purchased the Honda in 1974 (while we were at Towson) because of the gasoline crisis (the Honda yielded 30 miles per gallon). On gasoline-purchasing days, I would be out of bed, into the Olds carrying my breakfast, and in the filling station waiting line by 5:00 a.m. I would eat breakfast and take a nap until the filling station opened at 8:00 a.m. (By that time, the waiting line would often be one mile long, with me near the front.) I would then fill up the Olds' gasoline tank and drive it back home to park while I drove the Honda to school. I used the Olds as a tanker, siphoning gasoline to fill up the Honda tank as needed. Gasoline prices rose to more than one dollar per gallon for the first time, and news broadcasters on TV said that we would never see one dollar per gallon prices again.

On March 28, 1979, I was driving the Honda on an errand near LVC when suddenly the engine froze. I instantly stepped on the clutch, disengaging the transmission, and coasted to a stop. I had to have the car towed to a garage in Lebanon, Pennsylvania, to arrange for repairs. (The timing belt had broken, allowing the valves to be smashed by the pistons, scattering bits of valves throughout the engine.) While waiting for service, I heard a radio news announcer saying that there had been a malfunction in the nuclear power plant at Three Mile Island, approximately twenty miles away. While some interruption and inconvenience were expected, the public was in no danger, and the malfunction would be corrected quickly. I was not greatly concerned since I was accustomed to working with H-bombs in the Air Force with no history of unexpected incidents. I assumed that the nuclear plant had highly-trained personnel with the same sort of checks and counterchecks we used in the Air Force to ensure safety. As the whole world was soon to find out, the assumption was far from correct.

Eventually, the public learned that a cooling pump in the nuclear plant had shut down unexpectedly and that the minor mechanical failure had been escalated by multiple errors made by plant operators. For several days, the news broadcasters discussed the situation and gave predictions of possible outcomes, including nuclear meltdown. People in surrounding communities became more and more alarmed. Widespread panic was the result.

Lebanon Valley College had students from many locations where parents heard about the nuclear malfunction on network news broadcasts. Their immediate reaction was to call the students and say, "Come home." This the students did, with devastating effects upon our already small enrollment.

Many businesses in the towns near Three Mile Island were promptly closed and boarded up. Whole city blocks were closed, and very little business of any kind was conducted. Farmers in panic slaughtered all their livestock wherever they happened to be, loaded their cars or trucks with clothing and food, took their families with them, and left.

Somehow I kept working at LVC. We performed our scheduled concerts, our daughter Patricia (a student at LVC where children of faculty members received free tuition) made plans to spend a school year in Spain, and our son Ernest (music major) performed his junior recital on violin very successfully. Our youngest son, Edward Scott, was a high school student in Annville, where he was a fine baseball pitcher and my violin student. He created a sensation when he played a baseball game one afternoon and (without time for a shower) performed the first movement of Wieniawski Violin Concerto in a recital that evening. I almost couldn't believe this was possible, but he did it! I thoroughly enjoyed hearing the Concerto, being at the same time happy to be upwind of him.

When my yearly contract was issued, I discovered that mine was a terminal contract for one year (I was not tenured). This meant that I must find a new position during the next year, a difficult undertaking under the economic and social conditions of the time. I was not much surprised: all the warning signs were there. I requested and was granted permission to resign as of the end of the next year, brought my credentials up to date, and began searching for a new location.

Leaving LVC was a sad event for me and for my wife, Teena. We loved the school regardless of some serious weaknesses, and we had many cherished friends there. It was the third church-related college where I had taught, and I thought that such schools *should* be good. (Is it a modern example of the ancient disagreement between essence and existence?) I often heard that the most dangerous position to hold was that of administrator in a church-related liberal arts college, but I still like the idea of teaching in such a school. Perhaps at some time, I will meet someone who has had such a career and is truly happy with it. I would like to talk with that person, hoping to discover what I had been missing.

Finding a new position was a slow process under the circumstances, probably because of the economic conditions, the changes in culture (especially music) that were taking place, the time of year (most vacancies in college faculties seem to take place just before school begins in the fall), and my age (forty-seven). I had excellent credentials with recommendations from some very prominent musicians and administrators, but college search committees seem to gravitate toward younger faculty members. Perhaps this is because the younger "new hire" may accept lower rank and salary along with duties not consistent with the experience of senior level faculty members. Younger faculty members may be more popular with students, and benefits may cost the college less. The cost of medical benefits has soared in recent years, and older faculty members may represent greater risks in this area. In 1979, white males were disadvantaged because of increasing interest in balancing college faculties racially and sexually. In some cases, experience and reputation may offset these considerations, making some opportunities available to the older white male applicant. Finding the right match is the real challenge.

Rather late in the summer, I received three definite offers: a one-year replacement position at Moorhead (Minnesota) State University, a permanent position at the University of Natal in South Africa

(Durban/Pietermaritzburg), and a permanent position at University of Montgomery (Alabama). Since it was so late in the summer, I immediately signed a contract with Moorhead State University, the first definite offer I received.

While we were loading our moving van, I received a call from the Music chairperson of University of Montgomery. He said that he definitely wanted me to move to that school, but that he was required to interview prospective faculty members in person before he could offer a contract. I was very much interested in the position, but I explained that I already had a contract with MSU. If he could send me a contract, I would call MSU and try to resign, but I would not violate a contract. He was unable to do that. I have often wondered whether I should have made an exception in that case.

A few weeks later, I was appointed by the Ministry of Education in London, England, to teach in South Africa. I wondered how this could be and was informed that appointments came from the English while administration came from the Dutch. Sometimes this led to conflicts and cross-purposes, but that was the system. I was to take up my position the following year, so it seemed that my one-year position at MSU was fortuitous. I would have a year to prepare for the new adventure in South Africa, which I anticipated eagerly.

A permanent move to South Africa was indeed a large undertaking! (The administration at University of Natal used the word *undertaking* to mean our word *contract*, which I didn't understand. I didn't know quite what to do when they asked me to sign and return an "undertaking"!) I told a few friends about our plans, and most of them were quite concerned. South Africa was embroiled in the struggle to end apartheid, and appalling stories of events there were in the news often. A dear friend, Sister Josepha of the Carmelite Monastery in California, told us that she prayed daily that we would not go to South Africa because of the danger there. I found this hard to understand: if we could risk our lives honorably in the military, why should we hesitate to take the risks involved in teaching (which I considered of greater and more permanent value)?

Teena and I found as much literature about South Africa as we could find. We were fascinated to discover that Durban was near the Indian Ocean, the climate was much like that of San Francisco (California), and that Durban was a modern, attractive city. We also read rumors that absolutely anything was available there to a person with enough money. (We had seen examples in movies where assassins preparing to end the lives of prominent people would go to Durban to order special guns and equipment.) Added to this rather disconcerting information was the description of the area through which I would commute weekly from Durban to Pietermaritzburg: it was the home of Zulus, one of whose favorite artistic endeavors was head-shrinking. However, the same sources claimed that this activity was becoming unpopular and that head-shrinking was no longer likely to occur. (I felt that my head was about the right size already.) We were gratified to learn this, along with the information that the University of South Africa had been integrated for many years. This considerably alleviated our concern for the problems of apartheid, Sister Josepha's prayers notwithstanding.

We finished loading our moving van, hitched our Volkswagen Rabbit on the back, and began our trip to Moorhead, Minnesota, on one of the most beautiful days we could remember. Edward Scott, our youngest son, rode in the seat of the truck with Teena and me. Our dog and parakeet, properly caged, rode in the VW, the front wheels of which were in a special towing trailer. As we left the mountains of central Pennsylvania, Teena looked back and said that they seemed to be calling us to return, holding out their arms to embrace us. Our vision was somewhat dimmed for a while as we struggled to hold back tears.

29

I had scarcely given a second thought to our plan to drive a twenty-four foot U-Haul from Pennsylvania to Minnesota! I had years of automobile driving to my credit plus years of piloting such aircraft as the B-47, the C-119, and smaller craft. How difficult could it be to drive a moving van with untold miles on its speedometer, a "stick" shift, all our material property loaded on it, my wife and son in the cab with me, our VW Rabbit hitched behind with our dog and our parakeet inside? I soon found out!

First, there was the matter of getting out of our driveway in Pennsylvania. We had built our house on a scenic lot in Mt. Gretna, with ample room in the driveway for any car or small-to-medium-sized truck. After loading the van and hitching the car behind, there was scant room to turn the van and head it out of the driveway! I asked Scott (our son) to stand near the house and direct me, which he did very well except that he was not accustomed to the dual wheels on the rear of the van (neither was I). The wheel nearest the house was just wide enough to hang over the edge of the driveway and run over the top of our well. This created quite a bounce as the wheel dropped off the far side of the well (about six inches high). I was quite thrilled as a vision came to me of the van rolling over toward our house, possibly landing on our son in the process! A few seconds later, my heartbeat returned to normal, no thanks to my driving skill!

(I first learned to drive on my dad's 1929 Model A Ford when I was about twelve years old. He would have me sit between his legs and steer while he dealt with the mysteries of clutch, gear shift, and accelerator. Later, as I grew taller, he moved over to the passenger seat and gave me full responsibility for driving.) A "stick" shift was nothing new to me: I had learned to drive when there was no other kind! All I had to do (I reasoned) on the U-Haul was add another speed to the three I already knew. I soon found out that I also had to "double-clutch," a process that I will not even attempt to explain here. This worked fairly well on the van, but it had endured many years of various levels of driver skill, an excuse I made to myself each time I raked the gears.

Another useful bit of knowledge came after a few hours of gear shifting: the clutch on that old van required a lot of strength in the left leg! I wondered whether I would become so tired that I simply couldn't shift or whether my left leg would look like Popeye's biceps by the time we arrived in Minnesota.

The van had one gasoline tank that held thirty gallons of fuel. I estimated the MPG to be about seven or eight. This meant that we had to carefully guess the distance between filling stations in order to avoid being stranded, not easy to do before GPS was invented. I tried not to allow the fuel tank to be less than half-full because we found some filling stations closed or out of gasoline and because I didn't quite trust the fuel gauge.

We practiced what I called "preventive bathrooming," related in meaning to preventive maintenance on cars and planes. We went to the bathroom before breakfast, after breakfast, and just before boarding the van for the next leg of the trip. Even so, it seemed that about fifteen minutes after we were established on the interstate, especially if visibility was poor, traffic was heavy, rain was pouring, and we had no idea where the next exit was we would have the conversation, which began, "Rich [Teena called me Rich], I know you're not going to like this, but…"

We spent the first night in Brownsburg, Indiana, with my sister Bea and her husband Glen Whaley. Our relatives from Bloomington came up for dinner and a short visit. Teena's mother "Granny" Patton, her sister Pattie, her brother Todd, my parents, and my sister Mary Jeanne with her husband Virgil Stephens were there. All of them were anxious to know about our situation and plans, which we shared as well as we knew, including our opportunity in South Africa. They

184

were extremely doubtful about South Africa, which some of them knew as "Booga-Booga Land."

We left Brownsburg early on a Sunday morning. Navigating with only a map, we somehow managed to miss the bypass of Chicago and go straight through the Loop! When I saw what we were doing, it was too late to change routes. Fortunately, there was almost no traffic, so we actually saved time and mileage by taking the direct route.

North of Chicago, the plains begin. I had flown over them many times in B-47 training flights at five hundred miles per hour airspeed and an altitude of thirty thousand feet, but they look very different from a U-Haul at fifty-five miles per hour with its occupants anxiously hoping the next open filling station is near. Sometimes, the distance between towns would be sixty miles of level, wide, excellent highway and nothing else to be seen. We could drive at high speed, sometimes as much as sixty miles per hour!

We had heard that northern Minnesota is populated mainly by Norwegians. Somehow we expected everyone to be dressed in the type of folk costumes we had seen in pictures, so we were vaguely disappointed to see that everyone looked, dressed, spoke, and behaved much like us. We noticed one thing that seemed foreign: we saw UFFDA (pronounced "OOF-da") stenciled on the backs of chairs and benches and in many other places. I thought it was an acrostic, similar to those that were common in the Air Force. I tried to guess what words the acrostic indicated. (United Fire Fighters Dousing America, for example?) I asked at a filling station, and the attendant explained that it was a very useful word! It could mean many things, including surprise, dismay, disgust, or confusion. Its meaning was determined by context and by tone of voice. I heard it many times while living in Moorhead, Minnesota, and Fargo, North Dakota.

We arranged to rent a house owned by the preceding string teacher/orchestra conductor at Moorhead State College (later University). He had left late in the summer year to accept a position in North Carolina. The house was modest, but large enough. It was clean and pleasant, but we had some warning about the temperature in winter: all the windows were covered with clear plastic for insulation.

The front doors of many houses in the area were adorned with a sort of knocker called a Norwegian Door Harp. It looked like a small lyre with four strings tuned to play a chord and four small wood knobs attached to threads arranged so that the knobs would strike the strings when the door was shaken. I liked the door harp, and I bought one as soon as possible from a retired Norwegian man who made them as a part-time avocation. I carefully kept mine in tune, but most people didn't. They may have been surprised when I "knocked" on their doors, and they opened to find me tuning their door harps!

Temporarily, at least, we were at home! I heard that the college president had announced in faculty meeting that I had been engaged for the one-year replacement position but was not yet present. He surmised that I was late because I was circling the campus looking for a parking place. Dr. Pattengale, chair of the Music Department, along with volunteers from the department, assisted us in unloading furniture from the van into the house, which we greatly appreciated.

30

The Red River runs (north!) between Fargo, North Dakota and Moorhead, Minnesota. It runs very slowly because the land is so flat. (The water is heavily polluted from fertilizers and insecticides sprayed on crops regularly. Public drinking water is drawn from the river and treated. If a glass of it is left standing, sediment will settle to the bottom, showing what is actually left in the water. *Bon appetit!*) Actually, the river is what remains of Lake Agassi, a large lake that once covered many miles of plains including large areas of the two states. Centuries ago the lake ran dry, leaving flat prairie with about one foot of topsoil composed of the remainders of plants and animals that once lived in the water. The topsoil is very light, almost like whipped cream with sand beneath, a perfect growing medium for root crops such as sugar beets and for sunflowers and flax. The growing season is short but intense. Summer days are long, due to the high latitude, and temperatures soar into the eighties or nineties. There is little spring or fall, and the short days of winter bring extremely cold temperatures beginning as early as September.

On our first Christmas Eve in Moorhead, Teena and I went to midnight worship at the Lutheran Church. The outside air temperature was thirty-five degrees below zero F, with a wind-chill of eighty-five degrees below zero. As usual, there was little snow in the area but much wind. A few trees grow there, planted rather recently as windbreaks. The wind is still strong, stirring up the topsoil, and any snow that falls looks horizontal, thoroughly mixed with dirt. The mixture is called "snirt."

Public meeting places, such as churches, have an electrical connection for each car in the parking lots. It is necessary to have a block-heater installed in the car's crank case to keep the oil warm while it is parked. Without the heater, the oil quickly becomes almost solid, making it impossible for the starter to turn the engine. During the winter season, drivers wisely carry emergency equipment, including insulated blankets, heating candles, water, high-energy foods, and first-aid kits. Without such equipment, any mishap (engine stalling, skidding off the road, etc.) can quickly become a life-threatening situation. I knew of one lady who left her house during a snowstorm to get some wood from the yard. She used a clothesline for navigation, but somehow, she became disoriented and froze to death within twenty feet of her kitchen door. Walking in such conditions is difficult: facing toward the wind makes exhaling difficult while facing away from the wind interferes with inhaling. When temperatures are extremely low, snow feels like sand blowing against bare skin. There is a tendency to try to cover the face with a scarf or part of the coat. Disorientation is easy!

The climate in northern Minnesota is the subject of many jokes among the populace. "Moorhead is not the end of the world, but you can see it from here." "The best view of Moorhead is in the rearview mirror of your car." "There is a contest on TV that has as its first prize a one-week paid vacation in Moorhead. Second prize is a *two-week* vacation in Moorhead."

The Norwegians I met loved music, especially the music of the Lutheran Church. They were known for choral singing, and many of them could sing Bach Cantatas, Handel Oratorios, and other sophisticated choral music. They also loved instrumental music, particularly the violin. One of their favorite selections, *Saeterjentens Sondog (The Shepherdess' Sunday)* was composed in the nineteenth century by the Norwegian violinist Ole Bull. Composed originally for singing, the text of this song is about a young shepherdess who is spending the summer months in the mountains above her village herding sheep and goats and making cheese. On a Sunday morning, she hears the organ playing in the chapel far below. She longs for autumn to arrive so that she can return to the village and attend chapel with her friends. The song was also published as a string quartet called *Solitude in the Mountains* and as a violin solo with organ.

Ole Bull was immensely successful as a touring concert violinist. He earned large sums of money, most of which he gave to the struggling Norwegian farmers of Minnesota and North Dakota. These farmers had migrated from Norway to Canada and then south to the northern plains of the United States. (Ole Bull's help probably enabled many of them to survive, which makes him a hero even to this day.) Since there were no trees in the area, they built small houses of sod which they cut in convenient sizes to use as building blocks. They also developed foods that could be made from available crops and from fish. Some of the foods, such as lutefisk (lye fish) and lefse (potato tortillas) are still popular there. They are served at holiday meals, and they are favorite subjects of comedians: "You can use lefse to patch holes in your roof or to repair shoe soles."

Teena and I attended the Lutheran Church while we were in Minnesota. The Lutherans were very faithful, always in attendance unless "providentially hindered." One rather creative way of attending was practiced in the summer season: most of the congregation would spend weekends at the lake, about forty miles from Moorhead. They would tune their portable radios to the station broadcasting our Lutheran worship so that the entire lake community was, in effect, in attendance. One Sunday morning, I played Ole Bull's *Saeterjentens Sondag* with the organist. The person on duty at the radio station said all the 'phones lit up "like a Christmas tree." People from the lake were calling to find out what we were playing! This recalled the saying, "If you want to know how many Norwegians are in an audience, play *Saeterjentens Sondag*. Those who are weeping are Norwegian."

I had one experience with the weeping: I played *Saeterjentens Sondag* at a ladies meeting of the Lutheran Church. Several hundred ladies were in attendance, and when I announced the name of my selection I heard a number of them excitedly voicing their approval. After a few bars of the music, I saw a number of them dabbing their eyes with their handkerchiefs. I might have been unaffected by this, but it recalled an experience of just a few days before, when our son Edward Scott left home to join the USAF Strings. Scott (as we call him) had finished his junior year at Moorhead State as a violin major, playing a number of virtuoso works including a Charles Ives Sonata on his junior recital. Being selected for the Air Force Strings was quite an honor, especially at his age, but I felt that he was not mature enough at that time. I hoped he would finish his degree, but he was determined to leave school and join the Strings. I was very worried and sad to see him go. I somehow recalled all this while I was playing and suddenly I also needed to use *my* handkerchief, perhaps in sympathy with the ladies in the audience. This would have been difficult: playing the violin requires the use of both hands! I was able to finish and rather abruptly make my escape without too much embarrassment.

I was generally treated very well at Moorhead State. The orchestra made good progress, but I discovered that the talent pool for recruitment was very limited. I also discovered that the school had a long history of employing string/orchestra faculty for two or three years and then denying them tenure, requiring them to leave. I surmised that this practice was designed to keep the string position on the faculty approved by the state while using the faculty member for such duties as teaching Music Appreciation and other courses. This was not uncommon among such colleges at that time. The effect was that the string/orchestra position was subordinate to the band and choral positions, especially if the string/orchestra faculty member was untenured or at a low rank needing to be promoted. I was well aware of this and other campus political maneuvers, but it didn't concern me: I was preparing to move to South Africa after one year.

I was told that at least one previous orchestra director had imported much of the orchestra from the Minneapolis Symphony (later called the Minnesota Symphony), much in the same manner that I had imported members of the Nashville Symphony in earlier years. I considered doing the same thing, but I didn't attempt it because the travelling distance was more than one hundred miles and because the salaries of members of the Minneapolis Symphony had risen to a prohibitive level. I decided that my role was to develop the student players as much as possible during my one-year residence at the school.

Our son, Edward Scott was a student at Moorhead State, by far the most advanced violinist at the school. He served admirably as concertmaster, assisted by Virginia Watson, another fine student. Later a Chinese student arrived (from China) whose name was Shi-Yuin Gao. She was also a fine student who could have advanced much more rapidly if she had been more devoted to practice. The rest of the strings were less advanced, but they learned quickly if we rehearsed in a very detailed, deliberate manner. The brass, woodwinds, and percussion were assigned by the band director, John Tesch. They were generally very capable, but they preferred to play jazz and objected to the rather limited use of their instruments in the music I chose to play. I tried to compensate for this by choosing concertos for solo winds or brass accompanied by strings, which led to the opposite problem: the solo parts were too difficult to be learned without rigorous daily practicing.

The orchestra presented its first concert during the early winter season. The most impressive selection was *St. Paul's Suite* by Gustav Holst. The title had nothing to do with St. Paul, Minnesota. The *Suite* was dedicated by the composer to St. Paul's Girl's School in Hammersmith, England, in appreciation for the new soundproof studio built for the composer, a faculty member at that school. The *Suite* is charming, containing mostly lively music taken from folk traditions and featuring challenging solos for the first violinist. Scott played the solos with *elan*, and the orchestra performed very well.

After the concert, we had a party at our house, with the college president, several other administrators, members of the music faculty and other friends present. This was a long-standing custom with us, an opportunity to discuss the concert, make future programming plans, and enjoy some food together. Everyone seemed pleased and excited with the concert.

As a member of the music faculty at Moorhead, I was expected to play in the Fargo-Moorhead Symphony. Members of the Symphony were mostly faculty members from the University of North Dakota, Concordia College (a Lutheran school in Moorhead) and Moorhead State. Advanced students from the colleges were also members along with several music teachers from the public schools. The Symphony was an ambitious effort for that location, and the community supported it enthusiastically. We gave concerts of standard symphonic music plus a few rather adventuresome selections. I was assistant concertmaster; and Scott, Virginia Watson, and Shi-Yuin were members of the violin section. A select group from the Symphony played as the Fargo-Moorhead Chamber Orchestra at the University of North Dakota. I accepted an invitation to conduct a concert by that group. I chose to conduct Handel's *Concerto Grosso in g minor*, Milhaud's *Creation of the World*, and Charles Ive's *Third Symphony (The Camp Meeting)*. I was generally pleased with the performance, a tape-recording of which I still have. It was broadcast over public radio in Minneapolis. I consider Ive's *Third Symphony* one of the great masterworks of the twentieth century. It contains layers of familiar hymns, which I analyzed in some detail and provided to introduce the work to the community.

Along with other members of the Fargo-Moorhead Symphony I was invited to play Fargo Opera productions. We performed a number of operas from the standard repertoire. Performances were uniformly good, representing the appropriate periods and musical styles.

31

Messages

I don't know why I decided to copy performance tapes last Sunday evening. I could have done it before or after, but I somehow felt compelled to copy them right then.

Between 10:00 and 11:00 p.m. (Minnesota time), I copied the Ives *Third Symphony*, a magnificent fantasia based upon familiar hymn tunes. The hymns included "Shall We Gather at the River, "O! for a Thousand Tongues to Sing Our Great Redeemer's Praise," "What a Friend We Have in Jesus," "Father Whate'er of Earthly Bliss," "It Is Well With My Soul," "How Happy Every Child of Grace," "There is a Happy Land Far Far Away," "I've Reached the Land of Corn and Wine," and "Just As I Am Without One Plea."

I awoke at 6:38 a.m. with the thought: *What would I do if I knew that someone I loved had only a few minutes or a few hours to live? Would I try to call or visit them? What would I say? How many times had I neglected to say or otherwise show how much I loved my family and friends?* I began to pray, as I often do when I awake at night and cannot sleep. I mentioned my family and friends by name, thanking the Heavenly Father for their lives and asking for protection, guidance, and care. I fell asleep praying, as I often do, but I haven't felt guilty about this since a minister-friend in Pennsylvania told me, "That's God's way of telling you you're tired!"

In a short time, the telephone rang and I was told that Dad had a heart attack the evening before between ten and eleven, and that he was in critical condition. At 11:00 a.m. the phone rang in my office with the news that he had died. I will always believe that Dad was speaking to me that night.

Just as I am, without one plea
But that Thy blood was shed for me
And that Thou bidd'st me come to Thee
O Lamb of God, I come.

Footprints

When I remember Dad, I tend to think of footprints. He used to plow rows in the garden when I was about three years old. As he pushed his small hand-plow, I would walk behind with a bucket of seeds, dropping them in the row spaced as he showed me.

We attended church regularly, and I loved the hymns we sang. I tended to connect them with everyday life, and Footprints of Jesus somehow came to be associated with my walking in Dad's footprints.

We used to be up before daybreak in winter to feed the livestock and gather wood for the day so that Dad could leave for work. I carried the kerosene lantern so that he could see. Usually, the pathway would be covered with snow, which had become ice in Dad's footprints. As we would walk along, I would try to stay in his footprints to keep my feet and clothing dry.

For me the "cold, dark mountain" was the stone bluff across the creek where we gathered wood for the stove and water for the dogs and pigs. As we walked along, I saw all sorts of imaginary shapes by the flickering lantern light.

I remember how warm the barn was where the cow and horses were kept and how good it smelled. I liked watching the pigs eat—the sound they made cracking corn in their teeth was somehow appetizing, even though they were picking up the grains from the mud in their pen.

I can almost see Dad walking ahead on a particularly rough part of the pathway, turning to shine his flashlight so that I could see his ice-covered footprints that "make the pathway glow." His shape outlined against the predawn winter sky, he says with just a hint of impatience as he waits for me: "Careful, now. Don't hurt yourself."

Goodbye

During summer vacations, we always visited Mom and Dad several times for meals and talk. We would walk around the home-place, seeing the barn, the creek, the horses, the dogs, and the garden (always full of vegetables, some doing well, others not). Sometimes we would take the old truck and drive just anywhere simply to be doing something together.

When our visits would be nearly over, I usually would tell Dad that we had to leave that day or the next. We fell into a little ritual that made goodbyes easier. He would shake hands with a firm grip, both of us fighting back tears. Voice unsteady, he would say, "I wish you didn't have to leave so soon. Maybe you can come by for a few minutes on the way."

Yes, Dad, I'll stop by. Just for a few minutes—on the way...

O wonderful, wonderful peace
Sweet peace, the gift of God's Love.

32

Although I had been appointed to teach at the University of Natal, there were many details that had to be completed during the two semesters in Minnesota. First, there was the problem of property disposal: we had approximately twice the amount of household goods allowed for shipment to South Africa. I had never thought of ourselves as very prosperous, but over the years, we had accumulated more personal belongings than we needed. Used household goods are not worth much, even if in good condition, and not many people wish to buy them. We are frugal by nature, not wanting to waste anything. For a short time, we were allowed to feel the burden of material possessions. A Vietnamese family unwittingly came to our rescue.

The Lutheran Church in Moorhead (where we were temporary members) sometimes agreed to guaranty support of refugees from the Vietnam War until they could become self-supporting in the United States. A family of such refugees arrived in Moorhead just as we were trying to dispose of household goods. We loaded furniture, kitchen utensils, dishes, bedding, and other articles on a trailer and gave them to the family. There was enough for them to survive in reasonable comfort, and we had plenty left!

A more difficult problem arose: citizenship. We could remain citizens of the United States, but we were required to also become citizens of South Africa (dual citizenship). This was not a problem for Teena and me. We planned to remain in South Africa for the rest of our lives, but of course, we would not abandon our priceless United States citizenship! We were told that the Ministry of Education in London, England, was responsible for our appointment at the

University, but the Dutch government was in charge of matters of citizenship. We were able to obtain only a two-year visa, not a permanent one. This was a very serious problem: without a visa, I would be unemployed! South Africa is not a great location from which to find a position in the United States.

A still more difficult problem arose with our son, Edward Scott. He was planning to move with us to South Africa and to accept dual citizenship, but he would be eligible for the draft for one year and would very likely be required to serve in the Army until he was twenty-one years old. We had seen newsreels and published photographs of Army activities in South Africa in the struggles of apartheid. Apparently, whole villages of colored people were slaughtered with machine-gun fire. I could not be responsible for the placement of our son in such a position. Although we had planned extensively for a new life in South Africa, even to the rental of a house there, I reluctantly resigned my appointment. I still have all the paperwork involved: I can review it whenever I wish and wonder what would have happened if we had taken that road!

So we were in Moorhead nearing the end of a one-year appointment. I was offered an extension of one year (I had not announced that I was leaving for South Africa), which I accepted reluctantly. I didn't feel that I could undertake the kind of development program needed by the University without tenure, and the history of orchestral development at Moorhead did not suggest that tenure was likely. I remained there for a total of three years and was given a contract for a fourth year, but I wanted to leave.

I received an announcement that there was a vacancy for an orchestral conductor/string teacher in the Manatee County Public Schools, Bradenton, Florida. In 1955, I had been licensed to teach at all levels of public schools, but I had never *held* such a position. A number of my college students prepared for public school teaching under my direction (I had supervised their student teaching and taught several String Methods courses). I saw beautiful pictures of the Gulf Coast sands just minutes away from where I would be teaching. I was also interested in testing some of the theories that I had taught for many years. I applied to fill the vacancy. (The recent hard winter in Fargo-Moorhead probably influenced me to some extent.) I was invited to interview and was hired. I immediately resigned from Moorhead State University.

Moving from Fargo was difficult. Moving companies had many requests from people *leaving* the area, but few people were moving *to* Fargo. We had placed our furniture in storage in Fargo, planning to have a moving company pick it up, which didn't happen for several months. We had leased a beautiful condo that consisted of several two-story apartment-style buildings with ample room for us and spectacular grounds planted tastefully in tropical style and furnished with hot tubs and swimming pools in convenient locations. Many of the residents owned condos as retirement homes. Teena and I bought enough temporary furniture to survive until our moving van finally arrived.

The first thing unloaded was a snow shovel! Thinking that my use for *that* was gone, I propped it up on a palm tree and took a picture of it. I don't remember how we disposed of the snow shovel, but the market for it was very small.

My assignment was to conduct the orchestras at Southeast High School and at Manatee High School (intensely rival schools). I soon discovered that Manatee Public Schools functioned as much as possible like professional football clubs. Football was the governing force in the community, which functioned as a closed society. A highly-advertised orange-juice producer was located in Bradenton, orange juice was plentiful, and a large labor force was needed to fill all positions from planting to cultivating, harvesting, processing, packaging, and selling orange juice and related products. The orange juice company contributed generously to high school football in the community. *Music* meant marching band for football games. Coaches were able to control academic activities in the schools, including music. Teachers were judged by their contribution to the football culture. Most string/orchestra teachers were wives of band directors. Orchestra members felt free to skip rehearsals in order to participate in band activities. At Southeast, orchestra was regarded as a way for band students to eke out another credit per semester. Manatee High School Orchestra had a more independent attitude and a longer/better tradition of orchestral performance. They also had an Orchestra Parents' Club comparable to the Band Boosters.

One of the most active parents in the club had an ambition to take the Manatee Chamber Orchestra to New York for a few days of performance, concert attendance, and general cultural awareness. I was not overly enthusiastic about such a trip: I was quite familiar with the necessary fund-raising activities, careful planning, and supervision inherent in such a project. However, I was willing to undertake it because I saw it as a means of uniting the supporting community in an activity that could be identified as *orchestral*.

The parents, students, and many members of the community immediately began the work necessary to have the trip approved by the Board of Education. An agency that specialized in such trips was engaged, and an itinerary was planned according to the needs of our orchestra. We would travel to New York and return on a scheduled airline. We would live in a small, but attractive, hotel in the Theatre District for two nights (three days). We would perform our main concert on the first full day in New York at the High School for Performing Arts in Newark, New Jersey (a short bus ride from New York). We would attend a performance of a new musical *Into the Woods* on Broadway and a concert by the New York Philharmonic at Lincoln Center. We would also rehearse in a professional rehearsal hall with a professional conductor for two hours and play an afternoon performance in Cathedral of St. John the Divine in New York. On the afternoon before our evening flight to Bradenton, the students would be turned loose at the top of Fifth Avenue and allowed to shop down to St. Patrick's Cathedral where they would meet our bus.

On this memorable trip, our students ate at least one meal at the Hard Rock Café, visited the top of the Empire State Building, rode the Statton Island Ferry, and did other tourist-type activities. It was a very busy, very valuable, and very tiring trip. I mentioned to some of the parents that we took thirty-four students to New York and brought back thirty-four very different students! Safety was the primary concern during the trip. This required that students must be accompanied by a chaperone except for the Fifth Avenue Shopping

Spree. On that spree, the students must remain on Fifth Avenue with at least one companion, and they must arrive at the bus on time.

The Manatee Board of Education generally expected that students would perform at least one concert for evaluation when they went on trips such as our trip to New York. Our evaluation occurred at the High School for Performing Arts (strategically place at the *beginning* of our stay in New York).

After a bus ride, we arrived at the site of the concert. Our students went from the bus to the stage entrance and began to set up for the performance (with the curtains closed). We could hear the audience, and we knew it was large. What we *didn't* know was that it was all African American except for our group. (Almost all of our students were *white*.) We also didn't know that quite a few celebrities were in the audience, all curious to see and hear a student chamber orchestra from a Florida public school. The student body from the performing arts school was also there. When the curtain opened, there was an audible gasp from on- *and* off-stage! It is a credit to all present that we instantly understood and welcomed the racial diversity represented at the concert.

Our fine students performed brilliantly, and the audience responded with great enthusiasm! We received "I," the highest rating possible, along with some very helpful criticism. After the concert, we shared a delicious lunch at the school cafeteria, where there was an opportunity to get acquainted. I was surprised to be treated as a sort of orchestral *guru*. I was asked all sorts of questions about my musical experience and philosophy. One of the rather puzzling questions was, "Are you a disciplinarian as a teacher?" I wasn't sure what the questioner meant, but I answered that I expected all students to support the goals of the orchestra and to work toward the accomplishment of these goals. Generally, we couldn't do this without an inherent love for what we were doing. *Discipline* is derived from *disciple*. In that sense, I suppose I am a disciplinarian.

During my second year at Manatee County, I received a letter from the Atlanta Public Schools, asking whether I was interested in teaching there. I answered that I was interested, and I was asked to interview, which I did. I was offered a position to begin immediately, but I didn't want to break my contract. We made an agreement that I would come to Atlanta the following year, but if the situation developed, that I must move to Atlanta immediately or lose the position I would break my contract with Manatee County.

33

Teena and I arrived in Atlanta in August 1989. I had not seen the city since I left there in 1956. I hardly recognized anything. I-75 and I-85 had been completed, forming a "Y" through the center of the city, and I-285 circled the city. This made access to all of Atlanta rather simple and much quicker than it had been when I last lived there. (At that time, the city was like a collection of small towns connected by a series of narrow streets with much traffic and many traffic lights. Buckhead was a very small town, most of which is still in existence as a sort of entrance to the large city, which it is now.)

We found a new apartment complex close to I-85, across the street from Mercer University. Our apartment was on the first floor, with a private entrance from the surrounding woods in addition to a more formal front entrance used jointly with other apartment dwellers. The two-bedroom apartment was immaculate and quiet, and the university campus gave us an ample walking area all seasons of the year. We had a lovely swimming facility and exercise room, and the grounds were beautifully landscaped. Most of the other tenants were college students and young professionals.

My daily commute would be approximately thirty minutes each way. I had to leave for work at approximately 6:30 a.m. and return at approximately 4:00 p.m., times that allowed me to miss most of the heavy traffic. I had to become accustomed to high speeds on a multilane highway, planning entries, exits, and changes of lane to accommodate the situation and make commutes safe and efficient.

My duties with the Atlanta Public Schools began with orientation week. I was instructed to go to a large cafeteria near the state capitol, have lunch, and meet my supervisor. My assignment was to develop a string instruction program in the area from Georgia Tech to Morehouse College, one of the toughest areas in Atlanta. String instruction was a new venture in this area, and apparently no school personnel knew what I was supposed to do. My area included one high school, one middle school, and four elementary schools. My equipment was one dozen folding music stands (no music, no instruments, and no classroom). My assigned supervisor was the principal of E. R. Carter Elementary School, designated as my base school. (Gladys Knight, the famous singer, was a student there in her elementary school days.)

I was enjoying a delicious lunch when suddenly I was interrupted by a vivacious young lady who asked if I was Dr. Richardson. She introduced herself as Charlotte Johnson, principal of E. R. Carter and my supervisor. (I learned later that she was also a "doctor," and I fell into the habit of calling her "Dr. J.")

I had met Mary Frances Early and Arlene Witte, coordinators of Music for Atlanta Public Schools, but Dr. J was the first principal I met. I was immediately impressed by her energy, sense of humor, and commitment to mission. She told me something of her history and her daily activities. One of the fascinating bits of information was that she was a follower of Martin Luther King in the early days of the civil rights movement (when she was in high school). She laughingly said that she wasn't really that interested in the movement, but she thought Dr. King had "cute buns"!

Dr. J took me on a tour of E. R. Carter Elementary School. I was appalled and impressed in approximately equal measures. The building was very old, poorly planned, and in extremely poor condition, but it was cleaned and waxed within an inch of its life. Dr. J watched me carefully for my reaction to the tour, telling me later that she didn't know whether to expect me to laugh or cry. She had done both during her experience in that building. Perhaps the most discouraging feature of the building was that there was no space for string teaching! When I asked her how I was to carry on my assignment, she suggested that I teach in the cafeteria during the time when meals were being prepared and Physical Education classes were being taught! After we had an opportunity to demonstrate the operation of string class, I was given half of a temporary building for my work, the best available solution to the problem.

The high school in my area was Booker T. Washington High School, named for the founder of Tuskegee Institute and famous as the school Martin Luther King attended. The historic old school was familiar to me from reading about it in reference books, where I also saw pictures of its beautiful architecture. (Across the street from the school is an exact replica of Franklin Delano Roosevelt's Little White House, built for beloved musician Graham Jackson of the president's staff. We were told that the replica cost twelve thousand dollars at the time of its construction.)

I was advised that I should not attempt to start a string program at Washington High School, even though it was in my area. There were no string students at the school, and discipline problems were so severe that a string program would be likely to fail. An example of the discipline problems: the students enjoyed filling trash cans with flammable trash, setting them on fire, and rolling them down the stairs of the school. I was disappointed with this advice, but I decided to abide by it, at least temporarily.

I began recruiting string students at each of my schools, visiting every classroom, demonstrating the violin with music that was familiar to the students, describing my plans for conducting the classes, and inviting students to sign up (with parental permission). Students were required to attend string classes regularly, to behave according to standards that I gave them, and to do their best to learn assigned lessons. I could dismiss them from class at any time. They responded positively, and I usually had about three hundred contact hours per week. (Contact hours were calculated by multiplying number of students times hours of instruction for each week.) Students generally were excited to be in string class and wanted to remain there.

We had no instruments at first. I met this challenge by inventing "fiddlesticks." These were made from stock wood approximately one and a half by one and a half inches cut to the length of a three-fourths-size violin. Each had two strings made of chalk line spaced and glued in the same position as real strings on a violin. The sticks were marked with painted lines spaced as fingers would be placed on violin fingerboards, and there was a small cut-out below the strings indicating where the bow should be placed. "Bows" were maple dowels cut to appropriate lengths. Using these primitive implements, students could learn fundamentals of holding violins and bows, placing fingers on strings, and "bowing." As I said to the PTA at a meeting recognizing my invention, "And best of all, they are silent!"

The APS Carpentry Shop made three hundred fiddlesticks and bows for me. Their workmanship was excellent, and they coated them with lacquer, which made them look attractive. The lacquer also prevented them from becoming soiled by perspiring little fingers.

The fiddlesticks could be used productively for about three weeks of instruction each semester, which gave me some time to secure instruments. I put together a rental-purchase plan that I thought the families could afford, but it was not attractive to the dealers in Atlanta. After approaching every string-instrument dealer in the area, I finally found one who would accept the plan. He ordered serviceable instruments, and we were in business!

I loved teaching the children, and they loved being in string class. I was given freedom to choose what age groups to include. After experimenting, I discovered that the best time for "my" children to begin was second grade (although I had beginners from all grades through middle school). The students often objected when the time came for class to end, wanting to stay longer. Parents treated me like royalty, often making comments such as "I believe God sent you to us." I usually answered, "I believe God sends everyone somewhere. The happy ones are the ones who go where they are sent."

For the first five years, almost everyone I saw at work was black (students, parents, teachers, administrators, and staff). Since I was inside my white body looking out, I never saw anyone who was white. I began to forget that I was white! I asked one of the principals if he ever forgot that he was black, and he answered, "I am reminded every day! They won't let me forget!"

I certainly learned what it is to be in the minority! I was one of very few male teachers, almost the only white teacher, the only string teacher in the area, the teacher with the most academic training, one of the oldest teachers, and the one with the most experience. Looking back, I wonder that I found any friends at all. I also wonder how I could have been so happy!

To my students, I was something of an oddity. Younger students often asked me questions such as, "Do you have eyebrows?" "Could I touch you?" "What color are your (various body parts)?" I answered them as well as I could, until one day, I tried to answer all questions at once: "I have all the same parts you have, but mine are older and different in color." I illustrated this by bringing paint chips to class, courtesy of Home Depot. I asked the students to pick out the colors that matched their skin, then to pick a color to match mine. No student chose either white or black, all of them ranging from light tan to rich brown. I was a sort of raspberry in color. I tried to teach them that to refer to people simply by color (white or black) was dehumanizing as well as untruthful.

Dr. J was determined that her students would have rich cultural experiences in addition to regular academic work. One of her projects was to take as many as possible to see a performance of Tchaikovsky's *Nutcracker Ballet* at the Civic Center. She asked me to drive my car and take a load of students, which I was happy to do.

As we drove into the parking area, we saw hundreds of school children leaving school buses and lining up to go into the Civic Center. Nearly all the children were white. I heard someone in my back seat say, "Oh, look! All of them are white! I'm afraid of white people." Another small voice said, "Dr. Richardson is white," to which the first replied, "I know, but Dr. Richardson is different." That was a proud moment for me.

Dr. J was also determined that her students would attend class. Most E. R. Carter students lived in a housing project near the school. I often heard that Dr. J would go to the project personally to track down absent students and insist that they go to class.

A great tragedy happened to Dr. J and one of her second-grade students before I was assigned at E. R. Carter. In order to get to and from school, it was necessary to cross Ashby Street, a very dangerous crossing. One day, there was some confusion about the crossing guard, and a second-grader apparently tried to cross the street alone.

He was struck by a car and seriously injured, with his eyes knocked out by the force of the blow. Dr. J had to hold his eyes in her hand as he was taken to the hospital in an emergency vehicle.

I learned of another tragedy indirectly. I recruited a group of students at one of my schools, in the rush accepting one girl without looking at her hands. When time came for instruction, I saw that four fingers of her right hand had been severed. I told her that I couldn't accept her since I couldn't imagine her holding a violin bow. She was very disappointed, so I asked to speak to her mother.

It seems that she was born without the presence of a doctor or midwife, her mother taking care of the birth by herself. Her mother cut the umbilical cord with a pair of scissors, in the process cutting off four fingers of the newborn baby. The mother asked if there was anything I could do to help her determined little daughter learn to play the violin. After careful thought, I decided to try.

I made a cast of the little girl's right hand in plaster of Paris. Using this mold as a guide, I carved a fixture from pine with a Dremel tool so that her stubs fit into the fixture. I arranged to fasten the fixture to a violin bow with Velcro so that she could hold it in playing position. Then I finished the fixture with varnish so that it looked like a piece of jewelry. It worked! I wrote an article to accompany pictures of the process hoping some publisher would be interested in it, but it was not accepted. In the article, I said that Tenethia could "twinkle with the best of them" (referring to the song "Twinkle, Twinkle, Little Star"). Years later, I heard from her. She had grown up but still remembered the situation and still had the fixture.

When I arrived in the Atlanta Public Schools, the system was in turmoil. A new superintendent had been hired, and he quickly became the center of controversy. A movement was underway to remove him from his position. This was highly publicized in *The Atlanta Journal-Constitution* in addition to live telecasts of meetings of the Board of Education. In the midst of this turmoil, a column in the AJC called attention to the death of a retired Atlanta teacher named Louise Pittman, eighty-five years old. The column was in the *Lifestyle* section of the paper, written by Celestine Sibley.

Ms. Pittman had taught for many years in the APS before there was a retirement plan for black teachers. She was highly regarded in the community. On one occasion, she was a sort of mediator when a group of young black activists picketed a Korean grocery store because of what they considered inferior merchandise and rude treatment. Ms. Pittman appealed for calm and reasonable discussion, which resulted in good will and agreement on both sides of the argument. Later, Ms. Pittman's home was vandalized and looted. The grateful Korean store owners made up for her loss and continued to deliver groceries to her when she could afford them. Unfortunately, she had so little money that she bought few groceries, and she eventually died of malnutrition. Ms. Sibley appealed in her column for the Atlanta community to help arrange a funeral for Ms. Pittman since there was no money available for such an event. I called the number provided and offered to play violin for the funeral. I also volunteered Dr. Timothy Albrecht, Emory University organist and faculty member to accompany me. This was rather presumptuous of me, but we had been close friends for several years, and he agreed to play.

The funeral was in the chapel of a large funeral home in what the community called "our town," referring to the days of segregation in Atlanta. (The area was also known as "Sweet Auburn.") We entered the chapel in the front where the body of the deceased was on display. I had never attended the funeral of a black person before, so I was quite surprised to see how black she *was*. I assumed that there was makeup to achieve that appearance, and that the color must be customary under the circumstances.

Dr. Albrecht and I played music that we had often performed before, creating an appropriate program as we played. Among the chosen selections were the complete Handel *Sonata in D* (played at the funeral of President Nixon), *Jesu, Joy of Man's Desiring* (J. S. Bach), and the spiritual *We Shall Walk Through the Valley in Peace* (performed at the funeral of Bobby Kennedy).

At the end of *Jesu, Joy*, I placed a mute on my violin and began the spiritual *(When we walk through the valley of the shadow of death…if Jesus Christ shall be our leader we shall walk through the val-*

ley in peace). Immediately, the congregation of several hundred began humming the melody with the violin very softly, perfectly together, and with profound emotion. We were united in expressing our gratitude for life and for people like Ms. Pittman. I can't remember another such experience! Unexpectedly, tears began to flow down my cheeks so much that I was concerned that I might not be able to play. As the spiritual ended, several people in the audience said, "Amen, brother"! Added to my embarrassment was the fact that Channel Five was taping the event with the expectation of broadcasting it that evening on television. (The broadcast was preempted by a broadcast of the beginnings of fighting against Saddam Hussein. I will never forget the eerie green images of bombs blasting and antiaircraft missiles exploding.) The funeral was filled with spirituality and dignity. Reverend Lewis conducted the service with great eloquence, and Liz Spraggins sang "His Eye is on the Sparrow" with a mastery that was effortless, poignant, and beautiful.

This was my public introduction to the section of Atlanta where I would be serving. I intended to be there one or two years, but I remained for fifteen. In this funeral and surrounding events, I found the strange duality that was to mark my experience with the Atlanta Public Schools: in the midst of every imaginable conflict and scandal there were hundreds of excellent teachers, administrators, staff, students, and parents who were making heroic efforts to accomplish the purpose of a school system.

I was often reminded of the parable of the wheat and the tares (Gospel of Matthew 13:24–30 and 36–40): they grow mixed together, they are difficult to distinguish, and trying to pull up the tares (weeds) risks damage to the wheat. It may be necessary to allow them to grow together until the time of harvest when the wheat will be recognized by the grain it bears.

I frequently met and interacted with very famous leaders of the Civil Rights Movement during my first years in the Atlanta Public Schools. Shortly after arriving in Atlanta, Teena (my wife) and I decided to attend Homecoming Services at Ebenezer Baptist Church.

When we arrived at the church (early enough for Sunday school) we discovered how small it was and how ordinary the building appeared inside and out. It was already crowded, and we wondered if we would be able to find a seat. A friendly man suggested that if we would first attend Sunday school we would be seated for worship. He seemed to suggest it as a sort of bargain, but we had already hoped to attend Sunday school so there was no problem.

There were about twelve in attendance at Sunday school, which was conducted as an informal study group with an assigned subject for the day. Everyone had an opportunity to ask questions and to offer opinions, including Teena and myself. It was an interesting and worthwhile experience, not very different from classes we had attended in other places.

The worship was very different for us! It was extremely energetic, emotional, and spontaneous. At the end of the hour, we were exhausted. We were invited to attend homecoming dinner in the MLK Center across the street from the church. Being unfamiliar with the area, we needed help in finding the center. I asked a lady to direct us, only to discover that she was Coretta Scott King, wife of MLK! She offered to take us to the center, which we accepted in amazement that an international celebrity was serving the public in that way. (The menu was varied and delicious, introducing me to a new food: collard greens. Since then "collards" have been among my favorite foods.)

On another occasion, Mrs. Polite, principal of Herndon Elementary School, asked me to provide about thirty minutes of music for a visiting dignitary before a meeting. I was happy to do that, and I put together a short program of classical violin music which included an unaccompanied Bach Partita, some Mozart, and other selections.

When I arrived at the multipurpose room to play, I discovered that my audience was the Rev. Dr. Joseph Lowery. He had been escorted to the room and was sitting in one of the rather small student chairs waiting for my performance. We greeted each other, and I began playing. Neither of us said anything at all until the end of my short recital, when Dr. Lowery thanked me. Later, I wondered if I had missed an opportunity to talk with him, especially since he might have shared some of his experiences with me. I believe now that we did exactly the right thing, allowing music to be the substance of our brief communion.

I felt that the area where I was teaching was ephemeral, either because I expected to be there a short time or because the area was gradually being transitioned to business use. In hope of capturing some of the atmosphere, I spent an afternoon with my camera taking pictures to illustrate the word *irony*.

I discovered an empty field overgrown with weeds, but in the field was equipment for mixing and molding concrete coffin vaults. Several men were busily pouring concrete into molds, taking finished vaults out of molds and loading them on trucks, and hauling materials to and from various locations. The day was sunny and breezy with brilliant blue sky and puffy white clouds. The background for the scene was the Atlanta skyline looking fresh, new, and prosperous. Symbolically, the scene represented death and life, poverty and prosperity to me. None of the men acknowledged my presence as I moved among them, adjusting my camera and snapping pictures.

In another scene, there was a tumbledown building that had been a garage-cum-filling station. In the shade of its nondescript roof, two happy-looking men sat drinking Cokes. The lighting prevented their features from being identifiable, but the familiar Coca-Cola logos on their cans of refreshment were plainly visible. Somehow the cheerful companionship of the two men contrasted with the hopelessness of the building in a way that seemed warm and expressive to me. (Could that building ever have been new? Who would design and build such a building? What forces could act upon paint to give it that appearance?)

As I drove back to the school, I saw a funeral home in the most depressed section of the whole area. It was a small frame building in a very crowded area. An inadequate parking lot surrounded the building, the whole being surrounded by a chain-link fence with locked gate. (Across the street was a liquor store protected by multiple security screens, locks, and chains.) Most parking spaces had metal signs with scriptural quotations on them next to metal signs advising that parking was permitted only for patrons of the establishment. Dire consequences were threatened for violators. I simply had to include that scene in my collection.

Another must-have scene was a large, muddy parking lot with my candidate for the ugliest building I had ever seen in the middle of it. Emblazoned upon a large sign on the building were the words "House of Beauty"! A friend later explained that this was a business that supplied beauty shop materials for the community.

I took many photos that afternoon and considered how to share them with the community. Eventually, I enlarged about fifteen of them and made a display of them on the wall of the multipurpose room at Herndon Elementary School. At the top, I placed a large banner with a poetic quote from Annette Wynn, "Where *We* Walk to School Each Day." The photos and banner were encased in clear plastic so that they could be re-used for years (and they were). I still have the original negatives and small prints among my large collection of photos.

34

Great changes took place during my tenure in the Atlanta Public Schools (1989–2004). Population shifts, changes in administrative personnel, political pressures, and changes in philosophy were reflected in school closings, new buildings erected, and old buildings remodeled. English Avenue Elementary and E. R. Carter Elementary were permanently closed. Booker T. Washington High School remained unfriendly to a string program. My beginning students were percolating upward from elementary to middle school, especially John F. Kennedy Middle School. I was asked to add Kennedy to my itinerary, which I was pleased to do. The string class there was very successful while the band program floundered. I was convinced that the reason for our success was the continuity of study afforded by my teaching the students as beginners and providing a solid foundation for advancement.

Eventually, I was asked to change my location to Little Five Points, across town from Sweet Auburn. Because of the difficulty commuting between the two areas, I was assigned to Mary Lin Elementary, Inman Middle School, and Grady High School (all in the Little Five Points community). The community had produced string programs for many years, which made it fertile territory to continue development.

In my new assignment, I increased emphasis upon a program we had begun in Sweet Auburn. I called it Wonderful Wednesday. On the last Wednesday of each month, we did not have regular string classes. Instead, I engaged a member of the Atlanta Symphony to travel with me that day to all of my schools presenting a short concert which introduced the guest's instrument and demonstrated how it could be blended with a violin as a duet. The Atlanta Federation of Musicians cooperated, furnishing trust funds to pay the guests. Guests included a bassoonist, a harpist, a trombonist, and a flutist. During each concert, the guest played an important solo for his/her instrument, we played a challenging duet, and we played some fun music just for entertainment. The audience consisted of students who did not have any disciplinary problems for that month. At first, we had small audiences, but soon, the students were motivated to behave in class so they could be among the chosen (practically the whole student body soon after the concerts began). We taught the students acceptable concert decorum. We had a special room (with a teacher in charge) where we sent students who misbehaved during the concert. Also, students who were making unusually good progress in string class were invited to perform in the concerts.

Both Inman Middle School and Grady High School were remodeled and greatly enlarged during my tenure. These welcome events were extremely inconvenient at the time because of the noise, the dust, and the improvised spaces for teaching. The music facilities in both schools were greatly improved. I was able to use the orchestra room at Inman for one year after it was finished: the orchestra room at Grady was unfinished when I retired.

I worked at least seven years longer than was necessary for the best of reasons: I loved what I was doing. However, when I was seventy-one years old, I began to feel so tired at the end of each day that I could hardly do anything when I arrived at home. It was time to announce my retirement, which I did. I would work one more year in order to allow time to fill my position and make a smooth transition to the work of my replacement.

35

Imagine that due to some unforeseen calamitous event, all sexual activity on earth suddenly came to a halt. This would affect life on earth in many devastating ways. Food would quickly disappear from supermarket shelves since practically all food is produced by sexual reproduction of plants or animals. Mass starvation of animals would begin within a few weeks as barren plants and animals were consumed but not replaced. The beautiful blue planet Earth would begin to transform into a body whose appearance would eventually be similar to that of the moon. Certainly, this would be a newsworthy event if there were people to produce and watch the news!

Television and internet news programs are already filled daily with sexual references. Abuse of children, same-sex marriage controversies, and policy changes regarding gay people in the military vie for time and space with news stories about the economy, forthcoming elections, and emerging nuclear weapons in various nations. Under these circumstances, it is almost unimaginable that a memoir should neglect all discussion of sex.

Sexual reproduction is a simple idea which contains vast complexities that account for the seemingly endless variety of life on earth. There is a male cell (called a *sperm*). There is also a female cell (called an *ovum* or *egg)*. New life begins with the union of a male and a female cell. Of all the cells that have been created in this manner no two identical cells have been discovered. (I like to think that the *ability* of creatures to reproduce is an *invitation to participate* in creation.) New creatures with endless variety have the best possible opportunity to be healthy.

The process by which the egg and the sperm are brought together is called *sex*. It is not necessary to discuss the mechanics of sexual behavior here. Discussions, photos, and videos are almost ubiquitous and inescapable by anyone who has a computer or a television set. Books and magazines are obsessed with it. Most popular music has sex as its primary topic. Sex is a primary or secondary subject of much art, great and not so great. It is sufficient to say that the variety and ingenuity of sexual behaviors are astonishing and entertaining, but they seem to have one primary purpose: the union of egg and sperm.

Human beings and some animals like to adorn sexual activity with all sorts of elaborations beyond those necessary for reproduction. Under favorable conditions, sexual activity is intensely enjoyable, perhaps one of the strongest drives experienced by all animals. (We don't know about plants, but they don't seem to be complaining: their most beautiful parts are organs of reproduction.) Aesthetic, military, religious, and sexual experiences are apparently closely related. The Roman Catholic Church has taught for hundreds of years that many forms of sexual caressing are acceptable in a married relationship provided that they result in placing sperm where it can fertilize an egg. Other organizations often have less stringent limitations.

I grew up on my parents' small farm, where we were vitally concerned with the reproduction of plants and animals, so I observed this process daily in many forms. It was sometimes my task to lead a cow to the neighbor's farm to be "served" by his bull. (I frequently recall the image of this process when I hear a politician or salesman offering to "serve" the public.) I observed and sometimes assisted with the birthing of puppies, kittens, calves, pigs, and other assorted animals. I cut seed potatoes into pieces with at least two "eyes" and planted them "in the moon" (according to Almanac instructions). Somehow, human sexuality was not discussed. When children were born (at home), parents usually did not warn us that this was going to happen. Instead, we were taken to our grandparents' home for a day or two and later arrived back at our home to greet a new brother or sister. We received no explanation of where the baby came from or how it arrived. When we discovered sex (we thought we had invented it!) at about age twelve, we were often alarmed and sometimes scared. We talked about it with friends our age and arrived at conclusions that were often wildly incorrect and could have been dangerous. Our sexual education was sketchy and euphemistic. "If you don't want to go to Indianapolis, don't get on the bus" (apologies to Garrison Keillor). Although I sort of wanted to get on the bus, I didn't know exactly how. I certainly could not imagine my parents ever doing anything like *that*!

Apparently, the ideal was to have children mature into adulthood with no sexual experience and little or no accurate knowledge. As we matured, we often heard adults surreptitiously engage in "smutty" conversations. One of my bachelor uncles, a veteran of the Spanish-American War, would speak about his experiences on drunken binges, usually once per month when he received his pension. He would spend a few days in Indianapolis visiting houses of ill repute (later I learned to call them that) and observing sexual behaviors that I could scarcely imagine, although his descriptions were quite detailed and vivid.

When I was in high school, I heard rumors that a Dr. Kinsey was doing research about sexual behavior in the human male. This research culminated in the publication of a book on the subject in 1948, two years before I entered college. The book was extremely controversial, but it was the first book that included reliable information about the many forms of sexual expression practiced by human males. As such, it seemed to fulfill a need among extremely ignorant people such as myself.

The ensuing flood of new information about sexual practices has had at least one good result: no longer is it possible to manipulate people by threatening to accuse them publicly of homosexuality. This may seem a small advantage until we consider that generations of young boys had been afraid to be seen carrying a violin in public lest they be called "queer." When my two sons were in high school, I had to provide each of them two violin outfits so that they could perform in school and practice at home without being assaulted on the way.

. After college, I entered the USAF as a second lieutenant. My first assigned duty at Lackland (Texas) Air Force Base was to read from the *Universal Code of Military Justice* to a group of new recruits on their first full day of duty. The assigned paragraphs to be read discussed various homosexual acts, describing them in considerable detail and warning that a military person found guilty of such acts would be sentenced to death by firing squad! I am sure that the UCMJ has been revised drastically since 1956, and people of my age may find it difficult to adjust our attitudes to keep up with currently accepted practices, which might be summarized: "Don't shoot 'em! Recruit 'em!"

For more than fifty years, I have taught students aged two to more than sixty years, with most of them of college age. I love being associated with young people, and I find great delight in watching them mature. I envy their enjoyment of life at their age level, and I feel saddened when I see them engaged in behaviors that endanger their health, happiness, and promise of success.

Sexual behavior seems to be more problematic to young students than any other activity. (In one of my middle schools in Atlanta, there was an average of one teenage pregnancy each month. We had at least one girl who "mooned" during her walks to classes every day. Several middle-school student girls would routinely drag boys into the girls' second-story restroom and molest them. I am not sure whether this was consensual, but it seemed inappropriate.) I believe this behavior results from the fact that in their short lives they have inherited a hopeless jumble of misinformation, outmoded and inconsistent standards of behavior, manipulation, and exploitation. This combined with a daily routine of cruelty and abuse could easily lead them into a belief that the only enjoyable activity available to them is sex. Many of them, often as young as fourteen years, resort to "getting pregnant" as a means of "opening their own case" with the welfare department. I have known several twenty-five-year-old grandmothers, themselves without husbands, who were bringing up grandchildren abandoned by their daughters.

The study of music affords an opportunity to learn about the relationship of aesthetic, spiritual, and sexual experience. In the book

A History of Musical Instruments, the author, Curt Sachs, describes primitive tribal practices regarding music. To summarize: musical instruments have sexual symbolism. Shell-shaped instruments, such as the violin, are feminine symbols because of the association of shells with the sea, whose tides are controlled by the moon, which is associated with the menstrual cycle. Straight instruments, such as the primitive trumpet, are masculine because their shapes suggest the phallus and their sharp penetrating tone supports the symbolism. Because of this symbolism, nuns were not allowed to play trumpet in European church orchestras during the fifteenth, sixteenth, and seventeenth centuries: a string instrument called the marine trumpet or *nonnengeige* (nun's fiddle) was invented to suggest the *timbre* of a trumpet without the masculine symbolism. Dr. Sachs includes much more about the relationship between musical instruments and sexuality, which may seem like arcane academic jargon to anyone who hasn't tried to recruit string students from a group of teenage boys or trumpet students from a group of girls of the same age. In that situation, the symbolism seems alive and well. Parental comments such as "I don't want *my boy* to play no violin" or "I don't want *my girl* to play no trumpet" remind us that we may indeed be only one generation away from the jungle.

For further consideration of sexual and musical symbolism, we could study the famous *Rite of Spring* by Igor Stravinsky. Study the shapes mentioned, the sounds, the rhythms, the melodies, the dance movements, and the story. Compare these to the same elements present in football and basketball games. The similarities have suggested to many people that these games are actually community fertility rites as celebrated in *our* generation.

The Curt Sachs book has been required reading in many college music history courses. I recommend it to anyone who wishes to further pursue this subject.

I remember well the advent of Elvis Pressley upon the musical scene. Many people were shocked to see the blatant sexual gyrations that were included in his performances. I was not surprised: he was simply reverting to primitive expressions that had been repressed in "polite" societies for so long that they were generally forgotten. ("What's old is what's new.")

It is clear that American society needs to reform education, particularly regarding sex. The school music program is perhaps uniquely suitable to lead in this effort or at least to contribute to it. What a great opportunity for music teachers!

I believe that children should grow up in an atmosphere of honesty about sex. They will be relieved to know that their parents have discovered that sex can be fun, humorous, inspiring, creative, fulfilling, and loving. It should be discussed as any other important topic is discussed, with parents and other adults sharing their own ideas, opinions, and experiences appropriately. The vast supply of information should be made available to children at appropriate ages when they express interest.

I remember one principal in the Atlanta Public Schools who closed our annual required faculty meeting about sexual abuse by stating that every teacher should include sex education in routine instruction and in lesson plans. I also remember at least one faculty member who expressed abhorrence at the idea. "I hate that word (sex)!" she would say vehemently. I couldn't help wondering how prevalent this attitude was and what the relationship was between the attitude and the conditions in the school system.

Despite good training and best intentions, many people are tempted to engage in sexual activity inappropriately, and many experience severe problems as a result. The story of David and Bathsheba (2 Samuel 11) illustrates this.

Sexual sin is understandable and forgivable just like any other sin, but the consequences can be devastating and enduring. In this connection, I am reminded of the parable of the Pharisee and the Publican (Luke 18:9). This parable is often used appropriately to illustrate the importance of humility. (It *was* the publican who went down to his house justified.) But we must remember that most of the Pharisee's prayer was admirable. It was good that he was grateful for his virtuous acts and his avoidance of sin: his problem was his attitude toward this good fortune.

Sexual attraction sometimes occurs between people who seem totally unlikely candidates for such attraction. Conversely, some people who seem to be highly motivated candidates for *any* kind of sexual behavior have difficulty finding another person who is interested. It is especially ironic to see and hear such people condemning the low morals of society. *Without opportunity, there is no virtue.*

36

My last Atlanta Public Schools concert was scheduled for Tuesday, April 20, 2004, in the Grady High School Theatre. The PTA informed me that "something special" was being planned in recognition of my retirement, but I should treat it as the traditional spring concert of the Inman Middle and Grady High School Orchestras. With this in mind, we programmed the music that the students had recently performed in festival plus added music to fill the hour. Kevin Hill, our choral conductor presented three compositions with combined choir and orchestra between performances by the orchestras. Dr. Timothy Albrecht, organist at Emory University, served as our piano accompanist as he or his wife, Tamara, had done in every concert I conducted in the Atlanta Public Schools during my fifteen-year tenure there. I will be forever grateful for their invaluable contributions to the education of young people.

About three weeks before the concert, I had a routine physical examination in which it was discovered that I needed a rather inelegant operation. Even though it was thought to be benign, a small growth needed to be removed as soon as possible. The operation was scheduled for two weeks later, which meant that it would be done *one week* before our concert! I asked how much time off I would need to recuperate. The answer: three weeks. It was impossible to reschedule the concert so late in the year, so I asked Kevin Hill if he would conduct in an emergency (my unavailability). He agreed, and we went ahead with plans for the concert. The operation was done, the growth was benign, and I decided to conduct even though I might not be comfortable.

Concert night arrived, and so did performers and audience, trekking through a maze of boards laid down to avoid the mud produced by construction of our new music building. When I walked into the theater I saw a large audience, many of them weeping! I couldn't help thinking "What an ominous beginning to a concert!" We tuned the Inman Orchestra after I made a short speech, saying, "I can't wait to find out how this evening will end, but it begins with the great Inman School Orchestra." I was proud of the students' performance, and I began to have faith that the evening would go well.

The selections with chorus were beautifully done, reminding me that public education should be done as a community united to produce a culture representing its finest aspirations.

The Grady Orchestra gave its best possible performance of some challenging music. Every member rose to the challenge, playing in appropriate styles with good technique. (It is easy to overconduct student performers; in this case, I was able to relax and allow them to express themselves with the flexibility characteristic of good ensemble playing.)

The concert built to a climax with a very fine string orchestra arrangement of the popular musical *Chicago* (selections), composed by John Kander and arranged by Ted Ricketts. The audience had been very responsive during the whole concert, but *Chicago* tore the house down (almost literally since it was under construction)! The audience was on its feet, applauding and yelling. I motioned for silence, told the audience that we didn't plan an encore, but we would repeat the *Waltz* from Tchaikovsky's *Sleeping Beauty*, which we did. The chorus assembled in the aisle and did an impromptu dance to the *Waltz*!

Then came the speeches. Administrators, teachers, parents, and students expressed their appreciation for our work together and their respect and affection for me. Mrs. Muntzing (violinist Sarah's mom) officiated, alternating speeches with gifts to me. I received a heritage-type rocking chair much like the one given to President Kennedy a few years before. I promptly sat in it to try it out, breathing an exaggerated sigh of relief that the audience appreciated. A wonderful portrait in pastels was unveiled, done exquisitely by Barbara Robinson (violist Isobel Robinson-Ortiz's Mom) and mounted in an antique frame. I received a copy of the program that had been framed with comments from the students handwritten in every available space. Grady High School presented me with a beautiful retirement plaque. Then Mrs. Muntzing asked if I would like to say something.

Earlier in the program, I had tried to speak to the audience and had choked up. The emotions of the moment had been too much for me. Everyone knew that normally I was rather loquacious! When I answered Mrs. Muntzing, "I'm seldom at a loss for words," the audience roared with laughter!

I spoke to the audience, saying that I was proud of the work we had been able to do in Atlanta, but we had only scratched the surface. I was hoping that my successor would be much more capable than me, and that the orchestra would not only survive but also flourish. I mentioned that I believe we are living in the golden age of music. There is more music available in more styles than ever before in history. Also there are more opportunities for music professionals than ever before. The Atlanta Board of Education has sponsored WABE-FM for many years, and anyone can receive the equivalent of a college music appreciation course simply by leaving his/her radio tuned to that station.

After the concert, Penn Collins, one of our very talented violinists, helped carry my gifts and load them in my car.

We adjourned to another room for a reception. As I walked in, I saw two large sheet cakes with copies of my pastel portrait reproduced in frosting on them! Most of the audience was in the room, ready to receive cake, ice cream, and drinks. One of the parents walked up to the cakes with a huge knife and rather unceremoniously cut through "my" stomach. This reminded me of my recent operation (which I had forgotten completely during the concert). I couldn't avoid wincing.

A few weeks later, I received a call from Lois Reitzes of WABE-FM informing me that I had been selected as artist of the month!

37

"*You will have charge over an angel, to keep her in all her ways...*"
"Is this a dream? Am I talking to myself? Or could it be...?"

"*Does it matter? Let's concentrate upon the results!*"

"What results? I recognize the quote, but it is sort of garbled. Isn't that sacrilege?"

"*The author has the right to change the original.*"

"Maybe, but who is the author?"

"*Let's get back to the topic.*"

"Which is?"

"*You have been sort of faithful over a few things, I will give you charge over one thing.*"

"Always with the scriptures! I don't trust Bible-bangers, especially when they mangle their own quotations! What are you talking about?"

"*Surely you have noticed changes in Teena's behavior in recent years: lapses of memory, inability to do things that she formerly did without problems, inability to distinguish reality from fantasy...*"

"Yes, I've noticed these things and others too. I have some of the same problems, but I thought it was because of my age."

"*Teena's problems are different, and they signal the onset of a condition called Alzheimer's. Talk to her doctor, and he will probably prescribe the standard medications. There is no cure at present, but the medications are designed to slow the progress of the disease.*"

"But people with Alzheimer's die!"

"*So do people without Alzheimer's.*"

"But it's cruel! They lose control of their bodies, they can't remember their own names, they can't even recognize members of their family! They sometimes dress strangely and behave strangely in public! People make fun of them!"

"I suppose I will never understand the human capacity for cruelty! Some people seem to delight in the suffering of others, especially when the unfortunate ones cannot be blamed in any way! The cruelty of Alzheimer's is largely a projection by people who don't have Alzheimer's."

"That makes no sense to me!"

"Nor to me! Think of it this way: Teena may live a normal life span, with Alzheimer's becoming more noticeable as she ages. She may die of other causes, just like you or anyone else. I think of death not as the closing of a door but as the opening of a gate. There are many 'pearly gates' that lead to eternity. Alzheimer's is simply one of them. Perhaps the progression of Alzheimer's could be explained as a very gradual entrance to eternity through a gate that can be beautiful. For a while, part of Teena's personality may be in eternity while the remainder is on earth. It is likely that people in eternity can somehow be conscious of those still in temporal life, even if the temporal cannot contact the eternal. She may not be suffering at all during this process, even though you and her other loved ones may be in agony."

"How can I help to accomplish this miracle?"

"You already know the answer to this. Continue to love her as you have loved her for many years. Allow love to grow to the point where it is the dominant force in your life. Resolve to make every day as rich and full as possible, even though you may do only the simplest of things. Keep daily life as nearly normal as possible. Allow Teena to express herself as a valuable human being, not as an invalid whose days are numbered. Caress her, give her hugs and kisses. It is likely that she will understand physical expressions of love better than verbal. Arrange for her to have medical care as needed and to be comfortable. Talk with her about eternal life with the genuine anticipation that you feel."

"Thank you for patience as I try to cope with all this. I have just one question left, which may be so maudlin I hesitate to ask."

"Oh, go ahead! Aren't we friends?"

"Do you speak to an angel in a whisper? Or do you just say *I love you* out loud?"

38

When we lived at Uncle Virgil's small house near Unionville, my dad and I sometimes walked (rather than drove) to church on Sunday mornings if Mom and the girls were not able to go that day. It was less than a mile if we took the shortcut: a very pleasant walk, especially in springtime. I was four years old.

We would walk about one-half mile on the road and then change to a path that led through beautiful meadows filled with multicolored flowers. Small songbirds flitted from plant to plant, filling the air with their music. Bees added their buzz to the sound as they worked their way from bloom to bloom. Hundreds of colorful butterflies competed with the bees for nectar.

(Mom and Dad are now buried in our family plot near the former location of the "pole gap" entrance to those meadows. This area has become an expansion of Little Union Baptist Cemetery. I used to think that the angel Gabriel would announce resurrection with the blast of a trumpet: now I believe he will use a mellower-sounding instrument, perhaps a French horn in the key of E-flat. Perhaps he may play the hymn my mother chose for her funeral: "Each step I take my Savior walks beside me...until that day when my last steps are taken, each step I take just leads me closer home." An appropriate hymn for my dear mother, whose efforts in the hospital probably made it possible for me to take *any* steps after recuperating from my burns at age ten.)

We walked between the Baptist Church and the Church of Christ. We could hear the singing beginning with the Baptists, then mixing the two, and finally the Baptists fading so that we heard only members of the Church of Christ. The effect would have fascinated composer Charles Ives, who sometimes created similar effects in his music (composed in New England at approximately that time).

Our worship was rather lengthy, especially if one of our itinerant preachers was "delivering the message," as we called it. After about forty-five minutes, I would become tired and hungry. My thoughts turned to home and the wonderful dinner Mom would have prepared.

I don't know how she did it. We had only a small woodburning kitchen range, which we used winter and summer. Many years later, Teena and I visited President Franklin D. Roosevelt's "Little White House" in Warm Springs, Georgia, and found it was almost the same size (although much more attractive) and equipped with appliances similar to those we had when I was a child. Mom would often cook a large chuck roast in the oven, accompanying it with potatoes, carrots, and onions. The roast would have a wonderful caramelized crust, and the vegetables would be in natural gravy flavored with salt and pepper. She would bake rolls so light they almost floated in the air. Sometimes she also baked a cream pie or spice cake with burnt-sugar icing. This feast would await our family as Dad and I walked home from church. I could hardly endure until the service ended.

Communion was last in our order of worship. It seemed very long, especially since I didn't participate because I hadn't reached the "age of accountability." After the communion, we sang the final hymn, often "Lead Me Gently Home," a sort of metaphoric title representing both the closing of our service and the end of life. The congregation always sang that hymn with unusual fervor: their daily lives were very difficult and they had just experienced an hour when they could withdraw into a spiritual existence with people they loved. Heaven seemed so near that we could go there almost as routinely as we could walk home from church!

> Lead me gently home, Father…
> When life's toils are ended…
> In life's darkest hours…
> Lest I fall upon the wayside…

Lead me...
Far...
Beyond the starry sky...

"For the glory we were first created to share, both the nature and the kingdom divine! Now created again that our lives may remain throughout time and eternity thine."

Afterword

After our beautiful retirement concert, Teena and I moved into our nearly-new home near Young Harris, Georgia (in the North Georgia Mountains). We designed the home for ourselves, using a stock plan as a starting point. We were a two-home family during the last year of teaching in Atlanta, commuting to the mountains for weekends and vacations. The home is perfect for us, with plenty of space and a sort of rustic elegance. We have welcomed quite a few guests, including all members of our families. We agreed that we would like to have ten good years here: we have just finished ten and now are hoping for ten more! We are in generally good health, but we see signs that we are nearer the end than the beginning.

I planned not to play or teach after retirement; in fact, I thought of selling my violin and buying a boat! (Lake Chatuge is just a few miles away.) However, we remembered that we had owned a boat on the Chesapeake Bay during the years at Towson State College. We also remembered that we became quite bored with boating. Two of the best days in Maryland were the day we *bought* and the day we *sold* our boat!

Soon after we moved here, a little girl from Hayesville, North Carolina, called. She had heard that I was a violin teacher, and she hoped I would teach her. I explained that I was retired: she answered that it wouldn't hurt me to teach *one student*. I started teaching her, and soon I had thirty-two students! I also was invited to play at a number of community events (weddings, church services, and performances at Young Harris College). I enjoyed this rather limited amount of work, and I continue to do it today (with fewer students).

I also have a small recording studio where I produce a few CDs occasionally. Young Harris College invited me to teach String Methods several times, which I enjoyed.

The people here are delightful! We have many good friends who offer to help us at any time. About three years ago, we asked Fr. Frank Wilson if he could turn a couple of ignorant Methodists into brilliant Episcopalians. He replied that he would like to try. We are now members of St. Clare's Episcopal, and Father Frank is still working on us. (Ministers here have a problem: parishioners seem to feel that they are already *in* heaven!) Teena especially enjoys membership at St. Clare's, perhaps because it is small and everyone seems interested in us.

A neighbor (approximately our age) summed up his attitude in a way that spoke for us: these days practically all my prayers are "Thank you"!

Epilogue

E arly in July, Teena developed swelling in her legs and other symptoms that indicated failing health. The manager at Discovery Villages (where we were living) advised us to move from the cottage to Assisted Living in the main building across the street. We accepted his advice and prepared to move.

On the morning of the move, Teena was standing in the bathroom in front of the mirror. Her body suddenly began shaking violently. I helped her to sit down and called the office for help. Her condition improved after we moved to Assisted Living.

(We remained at Discover Village for about two months before moving to Charter Senior Living in Buford, about thirteen miles north of Suwanee.)

A few weeks after we moved to Buford, Teena was sent to the emergency room at Northeast Georgia Medical Center, where she was admitted to the hospital. She was diagnosed with lung cancer and congestive heart failure in addition to advanced-stage Alzheimer's. I was informed later by the oncologist that all available treatments were long and painful in administration and recover, and they were unlikely to be helpful considering Teena's age (eight-six). He recommended hospice care, which we began immediately.

I had no previous experience with hospice care, but I was informed that its purpose is to provide comfort to the patients while they live the remainder of their lives. They use narcotics primarily, here being no concern for addiction. I was given no information initially about possible longevity except that it was "likely weeks rather than months."

I was advised how to assist in treating Teen and how to account for every dose of narcotics (about ten kinds of them, each for a different purpose). The personnel at our senior citizens' residence were not allowed to administer narcotics. Teena was connected to oxygen, a great aid to her comfort. I was informed that Teena would receive no further medical treatment for her major illnesses, but that I could continue giving her the medications unrelated to heart, lung, and Alzheimer's diseases.

Teena and I had spoken often about the length of our lives and the possibility of death at any time. Our faith in God grew as we held private devotions in the garden at our residence, where there is a small shelter.

We could not go to church because of the COVID-19 crisis, but we listened to hymns and services on television. We developed the habit of kissing and repeating "I love thee, dear, through all eternity" from Edvard Grieg's "Ich liebe dich," which Teena's father sang at our wedding sixty-three years before. I began to hope that Teena might stay with me longer than expected. The hope was short-lived. The nurse prescribed morphine on September 10 to be administered by me very hour or two as needed.

On Monday, September 13, Teena ate a rather bland but nourishing meal without trouble, or so I thought. Shortly afterward, she coughed so violently I thought she might strangle. She had an alarmed expression, which indicated her awareness of the situation. I reported the episode to the nurse, who told me that whatever Teena swallowed went to her lungs rather than to her stomach. I was to stop administering anything by mouth. The implication was obvious.

On September 14, I was made aware that likely her last day had arrived. She was still semiconscious, but most of the time, she appeared to be sleeping. I administered narcotics as directed. I kissed her often, repeating our beloved refrain. Teena didn't seem frightened. I remembered the phrase "Perfect Love Casteth Out Fear" and realized that all I had to offer at that time was love.

At approximately 2:00 p.m., Teen said her last coherent words. She opened her beautiful eyes and, with a pleading expression said, "I'm very hungry."

I thought I was heartbroken already, but sadness flowed over me unlike anything I had ever known. I left the room for a few minutes. When I returned, the nurse said, "Teena is gone." Her face, fingers, and toes were white. I kissed her lovely brow for the last time. "I love thee, dear, through all eternity."

"The LORD cares deeply when his loved ones die" (Ps. 116:15).

In Celebration of the Life of Teena (Elpha Ernestine Patton) Richardson

September 29 in Blairsville, Georgia, was the type of day Teena loved. Early autumn coolness, scattered puffy clouds in a bright blue sky, gentle breezes, and hints of color in the leaves all combined to present the St. Clare's Episcopal Church we remembered as our charming place of worship for several years. (We kept our membership there after moving to Buford, Georgia where medical care was more conveniently located.)

Because of the coronavirus, we were uncertain whether the memorial service could be in the sanctuary with social distancing and mask or at the burial site with family members only. We were relieved to discover that we would be meeting in the sanctuary.

The service was very moving, filled with faith, hope, love, grace, beauty, joy, and peace. Teena's cremains were buried in what I call The Green Cathedral near our last Christmas tree, which we saved and shipped to St. Clare's about one year ago. Our names are engraved on the large stone carving near the graves. I hope my cremains will be buried next to hers, where we may symbolically spend eternity united just as we are spiritually united now.

The Gentleness of Your Hands

Honor her for all that her hands have done,
And let her works bring her praise at the city gate.
—Proverbs 31:31

Thank you, Mom, for the gentleness of your hands
That applied a brush to white paper and turned it from bleak to charming
With watercolor images like a scarecrow and pumpkins
A farm girl and her dog walking to school
And skating on a frozen pond, children with rosy cheeks and long fluttering scarves.
Your gentle hands carefully placed the needle on a vinyl disc.
And when you looked at us your brown eyes sparkled.
You smiled and announced, "This is the Scottish Fantasy."
Our living room in Baltimore with its yellow and gold shag carpet
Became a concert hall.
Not the kind where children must sit still.
In our concert hall we danced and waved our arms like we were conducting
This work by Max Bruch for orchestra and solo violin.
The music surrounded us like the highland of Scotland.
Mom, you were married sixty-three years to Dad, a violinist and music educator.
In your way, you were an educator too.
Your gentle hands turned for us the pages of library books
Full-page glossy photos of nature and national parks.

Subjects that inspire artists. You showed us their paintings.
You studied art education at Indiana University in Bloomington
The Midwest town where you grew up.
You taught us to notice form and color.
And you especially loved the paintings of Vincent van Gogh.
His birds fly over yellow and gold wheat fields.
His sunflowers remind me of you.
Autumn gold, white winter lace, the tender green of spring and summer's shady grove
You watched the tree tops from your mountain home in Young Harris, Georgia,
Where you and Dad retired.
From your artist's table you painted watercolor greeting cards
To send to grandchildren living far away.
With gentle hands, perhaps you paused to scratch Scherzo behind the ears,
As he lounged by your feet.
Always listening to music, your favorite song was "Somewhere Over the Rainbow."
A song about the home we yearn for.
You're there now, Mom. Home with your Lord and Savior.
We remember the gentleness of your hands.

Patricia (Richardson) Niemann

About the Author

Vernal Edward Richardson, born 1932, Bloomington, Indiana
BM and BME degrees, Indiana University, 1955
Member First Violins, Atlanta Symphony, 1955–56 season
USAF pilot (SAC), 1956–59
Assistant Professor, Music, David Lipscomb College, 1959–63
MM in Violin and Conducting, Indiana University, 1963
Assistant Professor, Music, Southeastern LA College, 1963–65
Assistant Professor, Music, Harding College, 1965–68
Assistant Professor, Music, Towson State College, 1968–79
DMA, violin, Catholic University of America (DC) 1977
Associate Professor, Music, Lebanon Valley College, 1979–82
Associate Professor, Music, Moorhead State College (Minnesota) 1982–85
Director of Orchestras, Manatee and Southeast High Schools (Florida) 1985–89
Orchestra Developer and Conductor, Atlanta Public Schools (Georgia) 1989–2004
Retired, Young Harris, GA 2004–present
Concurrent positions as concertmaster of symphony, theater, and recording studio orchestras, violin soloist, chamber musician, clinician, guest conductor

CPSIA information can be obtained
at www.ICGtesting.com
Printed in the USA
BVHW081623240922
647685BV00001B/4